NOB

& I DIDN'T HAVE A CHOICE

To tinda

Hope you enjoy the

book.

NOBODY ASKED ME & I DIDN'T HAVE A CHOICE

Surviving an Unexpected Divorce

RICKEY CARR

TATE PUBLISHING
AND ENTERPRISES, LLC

The opinions expressed by the author are not necessarily those of Tate Publishing, LLC.

This book is designed to provide accurate and authoritative information with regard to the subject matter covered. This information is given with the understanding that neither the author nor Tate Publishing, LLC is engaged in rendering legal, professional advice. Since the details of your situation are fact dependent, you should additionally seek the services of a competent professional.

Published by Tate Publishing & Enterprises, LLC
127 E. Trade Center Terrace | Mustang, Oklahoma 73064 USA
1.888.361.9473 | www.tatepublishing.com

Tate Publishing is committed to excellence in the publishing industry. The company reflects the philosophy established by the founders, based on Psalm 68:11,
"The Lord gave the word and great was the company of those who published it."

Book design copyright © 2011 by Tate Publishing, LLC. All rights reserved.
Cover design by Kellie Vincent
Interior design by April Marciszewski.

Published in the United States of America

ISBN: 978-1-61346-830-2
1. Biography & Autobiography / Personal Memoirs
2. Family & Relationships / Divorce & Separation
11.11.02

ACKNOWLEDGEMENTS

In writing a personal story, there are always people whose influence is never mentioned therein. So I would like to thank all those who helped make this possible. During the time I wrote the book, it was an emotional period for me. And many people were there for me in many different ways.

Some helped with their friendship and their time, while others were always there when I needed someone to care. The book doesn't tell that part of the story. But it is important to me that these people know they made it possible for me not only to survive, but to write the book.

First, I would like to thank my oldest friends Randy Wilson, Terry and Monica Ercanbrack, D. J. Basse, along with Dana and Laura Flowers. These people gave caring and helpful advice as well as kept me busy and sane on many occasions. They have been and always will be cherished in my memory.

To my immediate family of brother and sisters, our relationships have been enhanced due to their compassion and concern for my wellbeing. My sisters were always available any time I needed to talk or was emotionally distraught. It would be difficult to imagine how I could have come to this point without their love. My brother always seemed to call and ask me to do something at just the needed moment, wanting to make sure the big brother was okay. My parents were saddened by the event and the loss of a daughter-in-law they loved, but were always there with guidance, advice and love.

There would be no way to adequately express my gratitude toward Christy, Renee, and Craig—my children. Each played a role in helping their father emotionally and psychologically with their love, patience, and understanding. This was not an easy time for all of them and unfortunately my emotional state made it more difficult. However, no matter how bad I became, their love was always there. As much as I loved my children before this, I love them more today.

Someone who was a great help before submitting the book with my poor spelling and punctuation was Peggy Adams. This book might not have ever been published had she not helped me with my first submission.

Lastly, I would like to thank Jan Box for her assistance and guidance with the final writing of the manuscript. Her suggestions and ability at times to see what I needed to say and how to say it was greatly appreciated.

Of course, there are others who were always concerned about me and at times were there when I needed them. To all of you, I am eternally grateful.

THE WORDS

I don't love you. I'm not sure I ever really loved you, and I need out of this marriage.

These words ring in my head over and over every day. The day was January 25, 2009, a Sunday night. On July 23, 2009, a Thursday, I was divorced. At that moment, there were so many thoughts and emotions that ran through my mind. As I processed what had happened, something triggered a moment from a movie. There is a line from the second movie in the Lord of the Rings trilogy where the king says, "How did it all come to this?" I'm writing this book only two weeks after the divorce in hopes that my raw emotions will help me explain that last question.

We were married almost thirty-three years when I got the news that night. How does someone just stop loving someone after all those years and say that they might not have ever been in love with them? The mind begins to think of all the times you held her in your arms, kissed and made love to her, and she always told you she loved you. So when did it stop, or was it really ever there? Can someone really pretend for that long and be so convincing?

All marriages have their ups and downs, and ours was no different. I'll try to write this without bias and only tell the story as it unfolded. For I still have deep feelings for my former wife, and although it may not seem so as I write this, it is nevertheless true. Just because she divorced me, no paper or judge could change the way I feel. She has asked me many times to move on with my life, but she never ever asked me if that was what I wanted or gave me a choice.

When most marriages end, it seems the parties have come to an agreement that it is how it should be. That was not the case in our relationship. I never wanted the divorce, and on more than one occasion I begged her not to leave. We were married in a church by a preacher in front of friends, family, and before God, saying, "Till death do us part." I didn't know that meant unless you just didn't feel like doing it anymore. So what made our marriage fall apart? This is not just a *blame-her* book, for there was blame on both sides, but hopefully an examination of what makes some marriages come to this point.

I believe that there are stories in the book that may relate to many couples' struggles. Hopefully, by sharing my story, they will find solutions to avoid our final destination.

THE WEDDING

We were married, on my birthday, May 15, 1976. I thought at the time that it would be cool to be married on one's birthday; the advantages were obvious. First, how could one ever forget their anniversary? Second, that just meant more gifts and presents for me. In retrospect, this was selfish and a point of controversy throughout our marriage. The question: Are we celebrating our anniversary or my birthday? Both days were important to me, but how to balance them and make everyone happy was the trick.

When people get married, as a general rule they are in love. In our case, that was not exactly true. While we were very close and were each other's best friend, we did not have that. We got married in a fever of love. We had spent the better part of the two years after graduation from high school hanging out together, but we were not romantically involved. I dated several other girls over that period. The people we dated were people we each knew. This was a time in south Oklahoma City when we cruised up and down Fifty-Ninth Street looking for someone in hopes of getting lucky. But over time, people got married, moved away, and you just got too old to do that, so what then?

Getting married by the time I was twenty was always a goal of mine. Why, I don't really know. It seemed I was no longer a teenager, and if you were working and not going to school, it was time to settle down with a wife and start a family. Maybe it was having complete sex that was a motivating factor. Although, I had been with girls on a regular basis, I didn't want to take the chance of anyone getting pregnant. That was a different time, and the embarrassment it would have caused both my family and me was always in the back of my mind. She had never been with anyone physically until we got engaged, so perhaps her curiosity and hormones finally got the best of her. I'm not sure.

In case you may be wondering, we never actually dated before we got engaged. It's just that we were always together and she was always taking care of me in one way or another. She was like a den mother to a large group of guys who hung out at her apartment because it was the place to go. In the beginning, she had a roommate who at times had enough of us all hanging around; then a second roommate moved in, and it got worse. There was always someone there, and I was there every day. After she moved out on her own, there were still a lot of guys who hung around, but no one dated her because then where would the rest of us go? Eventually, it got down to just her and me at the apartment every day. Again, we were close but not involved. I even brought girls over to meet her as if I needed her stamp of approval. To say we had a different type of relationship might be an understatement.

Then December 1975 rolled around, and I realized in six months I would be twenty. I had better find someone to marry. For my part, this is sad, but to tell the truth, I was in love with another girl at this time, but there was no way we were getting married in the near or perhaps even the distant future, and our relationship had always been a rocky one; plus she was not yet eighteen. Her parents had plans for her to go to college, and a marriage to me was out of the question. Next, I went to Texas and proposed to a girl I had known for years, who promptly told me I had lost my mind and to go home. At this point, I wasn't really sure what I was going to do, only that I had five months to come up with a solution. Then in January, my former wife and I began to become more than just friends.

Depending on your perspective, our stories would be a little different on how we became engaged. It was late one night, and we were together in her room when I said that we should go ahead and get married! It seemed the perfect solution. We were together all the time, enjoyed each other's company, and were ready to move to the next stage in our lives. Now, I have always been in sales and have the knack to help people make decisions. This is where perhaps the stories would differ. She said I talked her into marrying me, and I would say I only pointed out the advantages and reasons why we should; plus, if you knew her even then, no one ever talked her into anything she didn't really want to do. So that night it was decided that we would get married on my birthday, May 15, a Saturday.

I'm Baptist; my former wife is Catholic. When I asked her dad for her hand, he asked if we were getting married in a Catholic Church. I said no and that my uncle was going to marry us at my church. Up until my former wife left me, this had never been discussed. At least, to what point she was upset about the doctrine of the ceremony, but it must have been there all along because it came up then that I had made it a big issue. She had never gone to Mass as far as I could remember, and never made any mention that she cared either way. Our children were raised as Baptists, and the only time we went to a Catholic Church was for Christmas Mass, which I always enjoyed. There was never an expressed desire on her part for the children to be brought up in the Catholic faith.

The wedding was at 7:00 P.M., with plenty of time for us to play in a softball game at two in the afternoon and be on time for the ceremony. My mother and everyone else about came unglued. What if someone in the wedding party got hurt? This was a possibility since more than half of them were on the field. Although no one was injured, Mark Batson, became ill and had to miss the wedding. Rick Visor stood in for him and had to wear a tux that was way too small. We had a large wedding, with four groomsmen and bridesmaids plus six men who lit the candles. It was a fun ceremony. She was as beautiful as any bride has ever looked with her beaming smile and long dark hair. I remember thinking that she appeared absolutely lovely. Some people were not convinced that we were actually going to get married; they honestly thought it was all going to be a big joke on everyone at the end, but the vows were said, and we were wed. The last part of the wedding, after the ceremony, was all about the leaving of the church. This was a time of hot-rod cars and wild chase scenes when leaving for the honeymoon. For days, we all got our cars ready for when we left. At the time, I had a '66 GTO convertible that was my pride and joy. When we came out of the church, my candy-apple red car was almost completely covered in white shoe polish and writing all over it. I could not believe what my friends had done to my "baby"! While I'm crying about what they did to the car, the guys kidnapped her and took her away! Wait! There couldn't be a chase, if I was not in front of everybody. So I threw my best friend, Randy Wilson, in the car and took off after my new bride. So the picture of me leaving the church has my best friend and me in a car that says "just married." What a way to start the marriage.

THE EARLY YEARS

In the beginning, with most marriages, it's all about adjustments. Some people live together for many years before they marry, and others date for long periods of time. However, there is still that time that all couples cope with in the beginning. With us, it was completely different because we had done neither of these things. So the getting to really know each other part came into play as well as all the other things that newlyweds deal with daily. She had lived out on her own since graduation and was very independent and still is to this day. I, on the other hand, had lived out with my buddy, Mark Batson, for about six months, which was a great experience, but he decided to get married, and I moved back home.

I still remember the first time she watched me shave. She seemed amazed that I could run the razor across my face and not cut it to bits and in such a short time. When we got married, we both had good jobs that paid fairly well. She was a bookkeeper, and I worked for a furniture rental company. It was decided that fall that I should go to college and get a degree in advertising or public relations. So I took a part-time job at Capitol Hill Baptist Church. This would be an event that changed not only the course of our marriage but contributed to the end thirty-three years later. I met a man named John Stringfellow who worked for an insurance company. John began to tell me how easy it was to make a living selling insurance door to door to people who owned or ran a business: work four or maybe five days, make big money, retire in ten years, and live off the renewals. This was too good to be true. As I said before, I have always been able to talk to people and show them how to make a decision. This would be like shooting fish in a barrel (to borrow an old sales expression), but what they forgot to tell me was that you still had to work very hard at it to make a living.

To make the situation worse was that I had to travel each week to Arkansas to work. I'd been married only six months, and I was going to be gone all week and leave her alone. She never told me I couldn't take any job, but I'm sure she regrets not insisting that I decline this position. The first week I came home she was so upset that I didn't even go the next week. They gave us time to sort it all out, and again my persuasiveness convinced her that this was the right thing to do for us in the long run. So I went up and down the street selling insurance, sometimes doing well and other times struggling to make ends meet. I traveled each week to Arkansas with Bill Trower and John, staying in cheap hotels to cut down on expenses. This was a life that not everyone could do and had caused many a marriage to fail. To work there permanently, we would have had to move to Arkansas.

Being newly married, a new job and new state was a lot for any couple.

A straight commission job was very demanding on the most experienced sales reps, but on a new salesman this could be overwhelming. Not knowing just how much each paycheck would bring would put the most stress on the best marriage. Some people need to know exactly what is coming in and going out each month. This described her completely. During our marriage, on my part this didn't happen often enough, and that was my fault. Some weeks everything went well. I worked hard, called on just the right people, and made good money. But more times than not, this was not the case and times would be tough. Many a month we were behind on our rent or didn't have money for food or anything else. I had always hoped she wouldn't have to work to help make ends meet; however, throughout our marriage that never happened.

After traveling back and forth for about six months, we made the move to Rodgers, Arkansas. I went ahead and found a three-bedroom house we could rent. We left Oklahoma City and headed for our new life together. It rained on us the last part of the four-hour trip, and we got to our new home late that night. It was a disaster. This house was a nice home, but it had old shag carpet that, to say the least, was ugly and seemed to her nothing like what I described. She cried almost all night and asked me to take her back home. I told her it would all look better in the morning and everything would work out and be fine.

Being gone all week has certain advantages and disadvantages. It was always great to see each other on the weekend. We spent quality time with one another, and we generally avoided conflict because the time was short. These weekends were perhaps the most affectionate times of my marriage. Being alone was never an easy thing to do even with friends and family around, but in a strange place with little support, it was almost impossible. I always looked forward to getting home, holding her, and being with her as much as I could. She was and still is a pretty woman, and I have always been attracted to her. The big disadvantage for her was just being alone the rest of the time and having to take care of everything while I was gone for the week. She paid the bills and dealt with anyone we needed to pay until I could get home.

We had friends that I worked with in the Trowers and Stingfellows. Every weekend we would spend time mainly at the Trowers playing games and just hanging out together. They are still friends of ours to this day, although John passed away a few years ago. I still keep in touch with his wife and daughters. Bill's wife and mine became very close, and it was a God-send for me that she had someone that she enjoyed being around. Although this was a difficult period in many ways, it was also great just being newlyweds and enjoying the fact that we were together going through this new experience with each other. You always think of the good times and all the fun, but there was still the other side, the struggles and pressure of living from day to day and paycheck to paycheck each week. Sometimes, this will bring couples closer together as they fight to make a better life; with us, it began what would define most of our marriage: our financial status.

To help make ends meet, she first went to work at a pizza place, but I don't really remember getting a lot of free pizza. The next place was a good job with the company that ran the retirement community in Bella Vista. Remembering the time frames of all the events from that time is difficult because it was a long time ago, but from 1976 to 1980 we moved to Arkansas and back home then back to Arkansas then home one last time. During that time, I worked for the insurance company and was an assistant manager for a clothing store. I always thought that I would figure it out and do the things I needed to do and be successful in the insurance industry, but in the beginning, that never happened and there was no one to blame but me.

Our finances started out on a rocky road, and for most of our marriage, that is where it stayed. The most tragic part of this time was that in order to get back home the last time, I sold our wedding rings, something she never got over and rightfully so. I never really understood how much this hurt her, and the fact that I never tried to go back and retrieve them was something she never forgave. I would make many mistakes in my marriage; this, however, may be the one that is the most unforgivable.

THE GIRLS

This chapter will be about our two beautiful daughters. Later, I'll discuss our son. The reason I separate the two is that because they were born in different stages of our marriage. Children always play a role in any marriage. Parents may have different ideas on how children should be raised. We had come from different family dynamics, so there were times when our philosophies differed. Our children have been and always will be the greatest joy of their mother's and my life. It is important to know who they are because toward the end, the way each of us had dealt with them became a point of conflict. In our family, we both showed them affection, but I was the one who always said, "I love you," and insisted that they say it back as if it was a game. Dad was the more fun one to play with, and Mom was the one who took care of things.

Each of the three had very different relationships with their mom. Now all three are very unique individuals, and that is a part of the reason. It is difficult to look back and say that you wished you had done more for your children, but that is always true for their mother and me. On my end, it was not providing them often enough with a lifestyle that we should have enjoyed; for their mother, it should be not being a kinder and nicer person to them and the people in our lives. Our children are like us in many ways; they are headstrong, opinionated, and outspoken at times, but each has certain qualities that are either their mother's or mine. So as you learn about them, you will see how their relationship with each of us plays a part of how the end was handled and the consequences that occurred.

Our first daughter was born while we were in Arkansas on June 11, 1978. Marlena Christine Carr was the spitting image of my mother when she was born. All of our families call her Christy, but her classmates and adult friends will know her as Marlena. I always thought Christy Carr was a cute name, but as she grew older, there were so many Christys in her class, and she felt that Marlena just fit her better. So she went by her first name, much to my dismay. From the very beginning, she was a daddy's girl and in some ways still is today. Her mother just thought she was about the cutest baby that ever lived, and she was a pretty baby with dark-brown eyes like her mom and lots of hair. When I was home, she went everywhere with me, riding on my lap in the car, which would be frowned on these days, but it was a great time for both her and me.

The Trowers had three girls as well, so somebody was always taking care of Christy. Her mom did a great job of always making her look pretty with the limited funds we had at times. She sewed dresses and made the cutest outfits. Halloween was special because of the neat costumes their mother would come up with or make for our kids. In her first two years, her mother raised Christy almost by herself because I was gone so much of the week, and when Daddy got home, it was play time. Affection was something she got plenty of as a baby from both of us because we were away from our home and families; plus she was our joy. Christy knew just how to play her mom and dad when she was little. She never played us against each other. She just would do or say the right thing to get her way, especially with Dad. Our favorite story about her was that when it was bedtime, she would go to bed and then wait till we were in the other room and say, "Five more minutes," meaning she wanted to get up and play. I don't ever remember telling her no. There wasn't anything that we didn't try to do for her when we could, and it saddens me now that I didn't do more.

We moved back to Oklahoma when Christy was one and half years old to be closer to both of our families. Besides not doing that well selling insurance, we were coming home every other weekend to show her off and see our families and friends. It didn't matter whether we could afford it or not. Moving home could give us the support that we needed, and I was always very family-orientated. We spent most Sunday afternoons at my mom and dad's with my entire family. When Christy was little, she was the only grandchild and the center of attention. She was always a happy baby and almost angelic at times. Both sets of grandparents never seemed to get enough of seeing their first grandchild.

Children seldom become what their parents envisioned. With a name like Christy Carr, she was going to be a cheerleader, head of the pom-pom team, or student council president, but that was not the path she chose or the one that was right for her. She was very talented in the things she did and liked to do. Being out front is not my first daughter; she is more of a behind-the-scenes kind of person who makes sure everything gets done. Christy is loyal almost to a fault and sometimes not one to forget or forgive easily. When she was little, she was afraid of almost everything: water, dogs, and cats—anything that was not under her control. She, as an adult, has overcome these things and has become someone who will take on things that in the past she would never have attempted.

We all went down the Illinois River on a family float trip when she was about eleven. Being in the water has never been Christy's favorite pastime and this trip would solidify that feeling. When I got ready to get in the boat, everyone else was already in and the boat had moved into deep water. As I tried to get in the boat, depending on whose story you believe, it flipped over causing all five of us to be in the water. The fact that she could not touch bottom was not a happy moment for my oldest daughter.

After everyone was back in the boat and we started down the river, she was a very unhappy and frightened child. But there was very little we could do so she prayed and sang "Help" as we floated merrily down the river. We reached the half-way point and she decided to stay at the cabin and watch TV until we came back to pick her up. It may seem strange that we would leave her there but the store personnel assured us they would take care of and watch over her until we returned. Christy was happy and we finished the trip. To this day she has never taken that trip again, and doesn't like the lake or swimming in the pool. Fortunately she still likes to take showers.

Christy and I have always had a special connection, as most fathers do with their daughters, but ours was always a little more than that because she looked like my side of the family. My former wife is Hispanic. With dark hair and deep-brown eyes, she was a very attractive woman. Christy got all of those features, but she has the lightest complexion of our three children. She has the face and body of my grandmother's family, so in many ways she doesn't look like her mother's daughter. However much her mother adored her, they never seemed to have our connection. The events surrounding the end of our marriage, combined with their past, made it difficult for both of them. Hopefully, in the future their relationship will improve.

Rosalind Renee Carr was born on July 4, 1980, and there could not have been a more fitting day. Renee is the perfect blend of both of us. She has my outgoing personality and her mother's attitude about getting things done, not only right but as soon as possible. She has a take-charge personality that has little tolerance for people who don't perform at their highest level. To give you an example, she went through college in three years and was a resident dorm manager, on the pom-pom team, and up for homecoming queen one year, so she didn't *just* go to school.

Renee looks most like her mother's side of the family and is our smallest child. The rest of us have to work at keeping our weight in check. She, on the other hand, has always been tiny. Again, she has dark-brown eyes and long brown hair, and her skin tone is much like her mother's. When we look at old family photos of her mother's family, it is obvious that she takes after that side of the family. When she was a baby, she was the mom's girl and had a special attachment to her mother. She and I were always doing things together that her big sister didn't like to do. I believe I could write a whole book on all the stories we have about Renee. Renee once jumped off the roof of a house we lived in around the age of seven because someone dared her to. The fact that she didn't break her leg or neck is a wonder. On a ski trip with the choir she went down the slopes where she probably should have gone, fell and hit her head. To my knowledge, she is also the only person in the family to have ever bungee jumped or really wanted to.

There wasn't anything she didn't like to do or try. She never met a dare she wouldn't take or a job she couldn't master. However, she was a child who knew how to push the limits with her parents. Renee was never in any kind of trouble because she would go right up to the line and put her little toe across then pull it back. She was our upfront child and hated to fail in anything. The most fitting story about her was when as a seventh grader she tried out for the cheer-leading squad and failed to make the team while her best friend did. This was her first real disappointment in life. After we talked about what she could have done better and what she needed to do to get ready for next year, she called the friend, and we all went out to dinner that night. The next year she made the squad.

Faith is something Renee always has had in her life. She believes very strongly in God and has never wavered in that faith, something that would come greatly into play later in her life. Along with her beliefs, she has a strong sense of right and wrong and almost never looks at things in shades of gray. You always know where you stand with her. If she thinks you are wrong, you'll know it right away. This ability to be straightforward with people has been a great asset for her when she has tempered it with understanding. Before her twenty-ninth birthday, she would be involved in something that would test her faith and compassion toward her mother after hearing the news that she wanted out of the marriage. Being a Christian person, this was something she never thought was right. That belief and her mother's determination to go at whatever cost, plus future events, would lead to their struggles with one another. Renee has forgiven her mother which should help with the healing process for them both.

THE FIRST SEPARATION

When the girls were almost five and three, we separated for the first time, and the story is much the same, except we stayed together. It is strange, the events one remembers of one's life, but this is as vivid as if it were yesterday. She was going out with the girls she worked with. I remember thinking she looked exceptionally nice that night. Never in my wildest dreams would I have believed she was actually going to meet another man. It was someone she had met through her job and developed an attraction to. What part the man played in all this I don't know and never asked. She was unhappy about where we were in our lives and that I was not the success that perhaps she thought I should have become. We lived in a small blue house that had two tiny bedrooms and almost no living space.

Since we had moved home, it had been a struggle for us financially because of my inability to find what I wanted to do in life and make a steady income. She, on the other hand, always had a solid job because of her bookkeeping skills. She is one of the most organized and efficient people you will ever meet. Her paycheck was always there every month to make sure as many bills as could would be paid, and I seemed to chip in with what I could to make ends meet. It wasn't that I didn't work; it was just that I was either chasing a better job or not doing the best I could at whatever I did, which was a major factor in what would happen later.

Up to this point of our marriage, I had more jobs than I should have had, and I just couldn't find the right opportunity or apply myself the way I should have. Being a success was something I always thought would just come to me in time. I was the type of person that everyone liked to be around, and it was assumed that I would eventually do great things in life. Success can be measured many different ways, but with us, it was about the money. Financially, we were not where we should have been. Whatever physical attraction there was between her and him, she just wanted a better life.

When she came home that night, *Hill Street Blues* was coming on the TV. At the time, it was one of my favorite shows. She said she wanted to talk to me, and all I could think was, *Can't this wait till after the show?* Then the bombshell was dropped. She wanted a divorce because she wasn't in love with me anymore. I asked if she was seeing someone else. She said no. It was that she was unhappy, and although she cared and loved me, she wasn't in love with me. Like I said, this sounds almost exactly what would be said years later. Saying I was stunned the first time would be putting it lightly. We had two little girls that were my life. She asked me if I could move out by the next day, so I packed up and went to my parents. Shocked and confused, I don't remember a lot about the next eight weeks, but I know I was a complete wreck struggling each day to go to work and to not think about my wife and children.

The man then told her for whatever reason that he wasn't going to see her. I never asked about this and never really wanted to know. What she was thinking at this point would only be speculation on my part, but I do believe she thought she would be able to find someone better than me. Perhaps going out to clubs and not getting any other offers right away may have disillusioned her. It might have caused her to think about how she would survive without help with the girls and additional money? Although separated, we went to my aunt's for thanksgiving with my family, where she practically threw herself at someone that was there not related to us. I took her home, and I told her that perhaps we shouldn't see each other for a while and left.

But I had to see my daughters, so we did see each other. I always tried to look good when I went to the house because I wanted her to notice me and win her back. One night I went to visit the girls, and after they went to bed, she asked if I could stay for a while. I wound up spending the night with her. I am sure she was lonely, and I was available and willing. We had a great time together that night, but I went home the next morning. Talk about confused. Were we getting back together, or was this a one-night stand? Since sex was never a huge part of our marriage, I didn't know really what to think or do. This seemed to be a positive sign. My mother even asked if I was going home since I spent the night there. I didn't know how to answer and remember saying I had no idea. A few days later when I got to my parents' house from work, my mother told me that my wife had come and gotten all my clothes and moved me home.

All I could think was that I was getting to go back to my wife and children. The pain I had been in for those weeks we were apart was gone, and I was going home. We talked about what happened and agreed that we should leave it in the past. I never once asked her if she found that she really did love or miss me. I just went home and acted as if nothing had ever happened. I promised to find a better job, work hard, and be the success she wanted me to be. Looking back now, if these questions had been asked before I blindly went home, the greater pain I would go through could have been avoided because as much as it hurt the first time, the second time around was almost unbearable. Why would anyone go back without knowing for sure? That is a question I can't answer to this day except to say I loved her very much and wanted to be her husband.

I was and have always been jealous of my wife though; she never knew this until the very end because I never told her. After the separation, I was always conscious of her behavior around other men. Although she never gave me reason to think she was seeing anyone, I never got over the fact that she had once upon a time. I have stated one of the mistakes in my marriage earlier, and I'm not sure how she views this after all these years, but it hurt then, and it hurts today.

Soon after we got back together, I did get a job that I was good at, worked hard, and got promoted to store manager. We were on the path finally that would lead us to the promised land of happy marriages, and for a time it was true. Another event would happen that would change our lives. The boy was born.

THE BOY

Randall Craig Carr was born on September 5, 1985. Describing Craig may prove to be the most difficult thing to do in this book. In case you haven't noticed, all of our children go by their middle names with the family. The oldest daughter was called Christy because I liked the name. Renee went by her middle name because Christy couldn't say Rosalind. By the time we had our son, it had become a tradition. Therefore he was called Craig. Craig was also named for one of my best friends, Randy Wilson. Randy's real first name is Randall, and my middle name is also Randell. We had agreed to name one of our sons after each other, but we didn't want him to go by Randy, so he went by his middle name like the girls. In retrospect, he and I both wish we had named him Mickey Randall, since Mickey Mantle was my favorite baseball player and he became a pretty good player and he could have gone by Mick when he grew older.

Craig was always what you would call a boy, meaning he not only did all the things that boys do, but at times he would do things so differently from the girls that it was hard for his mother to understand. Like the girls, he is a very independent adult, but when he was young, he was the one child who depended on us for different things. His relationship with us has been always split in that he did things with me and told things to his mother. We were both close to our son but in different ways; he was emotionally more drawn to his mother but because of sports spent more time with me. Craig played everything when he was young, except football. Although he was on soccer and basketball teams, his first love was baseball.

I'm not sure he even knew his name when he was young because we just called him "the boy," which was a little irritating, especially to his oldest sister. Craig came at a time when things were going well for us. We had bought a house, moved into the school district we graduated from, and our marriage was happy. He had two older sisters that loved to play and watch him and parents that at times made him too much the center of attention. Christy and Renee have always said that he was a spoiled child; that was never true, but because of the things he did and because he was my boy and his mother's last child, it may have seemed that way. To say that he didn't use this to his advantage, however, would be a great omission on my part because none of our children knew how to play their parents as well as Craig.

As a young child, he also had to endure certain physical features that were challenging. First he had an accident that caused him to lose several of his teeth and replace them with silver ones; plus he had to wear glasses at a very early age. He was a cute kid but hard to miss with those shiny silver teeth and big glasses.

I can't tell you how many pairs of glasses we went through when he was young. The only saving grace was that Greg Maddoux, Craig's favorite player, was a pitcher for the Atlanta Braves, his favorite team, and he wore glasses.

From grade school through high school, it seemed once a year I would get a call from someone in administration to come to the school about Craig. Not that he ever did anything that was all that bad; it was just there was some mischief he either caused or was a party to. Discipline with him was a point of difference with his mother and me because I handed down most of it with the children and especially with him. It may seem strange that the fun parent was the disciplinarian, but I was the stricter of the two. She always seemed to think more times than not that the punishment didn't fit the crime and that each child should have been treated the same. I felt that each child was different and with each circumstance the punishment should be decided. This was always a point of contention with the two of us.

Craig was never a mama's boy, but he was more emotionally attached to his mother when he was young. He always tried to do things that I would be proud of, but his mother's approval was always the key. When the end came for us, it was and has been the hardest on him because of his split ties and that through the years his mother had become a person all of the children were not happy to be around. My children love their mother; they just didn't always like her, and to a great degree that is still true. You might think it was because of the divorce, but that is not the major factor in their relationship. Craig and his mom have the best relationship of the three, yet he has had a hard time dealing with her because of my feelings and his mixed emotions. Craig, more than the other two, has been put in the middle more times than he should have been, and that was mostly my fault, and I regret that today. I'm sure she is saddened by the fact that, although he didn't choose a side, he didn't support her the way she thought he would.

The children have each dealt with this differently, but there will come a time when they will move past their feelings and work toward a better situation with their mother. We have often disagreed on how much our grown children should know and have very different views on this matter. I felt they should know all we could tell them about what was going on, but she only wanted them to know very little if anything at all, which is not what they wanted. So another wedge was driven between them and her. I tried many times for all of them to open up to one another, but neither side would budge. All of them have had conversations with her about this and about the past but never to each other's satisfaction. As a family, we need to remember the love we feel for each other is greater than the hurt we have caused. I always pray that day will come.

THE SCHOOL YEARS

This is a time frame from Christy going to kindergarten until Craig graduated in 2004. Our lives were wrapped up completely in our children and their activities. We were very active in all areas of their lives whether it was choir, sports, cheerleading, or any other activity. Going to anything they were doing was a top priority for both of us, and we almost never missed an event. Not only that, we were involved as coaches, club officers, volunteers, and financial supporters when we could be.

During this time, our marriage would see great highs and lows. We lived in five different homes, and I am not sure how many jobs I had during this time, but it was more than it should have been. As I said before, when the girls were about to start school, we moved to the school district where we had both graduated from, Western Heights. It was an excellent school system, and it was where we wanted the children to attend. When we bought our first home, believe me, we had no idea what we were doing. We just wanted a place that was our own. I was working as a manager for a furniture rental store, and she was an office manager for a beauty supply company. We both made good money and had three beautiful children and a new home. This was the life we had hoped for all those years.

I was with the furniture rental company and had worked my way up to manager of one of the local stores. Having been in this field when we got married, it was something I was not only talented at, but my branch was very successful. Everyone in their lives finds things they are good at, and this industry was an area I always did well in, whether it was running a branch or out talking to apartment managers. I had a knack of getting the business. It is a demanding field because of the hours and people that you can come in contact with daily. Financially, it was never going to make us rich, but it was a good income for someone with no college education or special training. Any time you are good at what you do it will make all of the negatives about the job seem unimportant.

She was working for a beauty supply company as their office manager. It was a new company at the time, and she was perfect for the job. She was there for over twenty years until they went out of business. Being organized and efficient doesn't even begin to describe her daily work ethic. As successful as this company was for many years, I don't think she ever really got the credit she deserved for that success. To the best of my memory, she may have only missed the number of days on one hand because she was sick or any other reason, except if the kids were involved. There were times, however, that she wanted to walk away from the job for a number of reasons but always stayed to make sure we had a steady income. I know she enjoyed her position most of the time she was there, but the fact that she couldn't go if she wanted to because of me was another mistake on my part in the marriage.

We had lived in our home for about two years when I was let go from the furniture store. I have been let go twice in my life. The first one I deserved when I was young, but not this time. Who knows how our lives might have been different if this event had never happened. Turnover in this industry was common. I had seen people come and go for three years. The regional manager I had at the time was not always the most likeable guy, and I can get along with anyone. Although my branch was successful, we were known to be mavericks. Now anytime you are let go, there can be two sides to the story, and I should have known that it was a possibility, but I promoted three managers out of the store and had good numbers for that kind of operation. My problem was that I was so sure that my success would insulate me that I never saw it coming. There are things I should have done that would have kept the situation from ever happening, but my ego got in the way. Because I was so good at working with apartment managers, a few years later they would bring me back, but right then I had a mortgage payment that was due.

The loan we got at that time had an interest rate of about 11 percent, which in 1984 was a decent rate. Our payments, however, were set up on an adjustable rate after two years, something I would never do now, but at the time, we didn't know any better. So I lost my job, and our payments were going up to a point that we couldn't afford the house. I have no real memory of where I worked at that time, but I know that we wound up losing the home. If had known then what I do now, that might have never happened, but we were still young and just didn't understand how things worked. It was a painful and embarrassing lesson, but it would come into play later. She took this better than anyone would have thought. The payment was way too much for us. Therefore, we were moving just down the street to a rental home that was within our budget. In addition, her sister Mary was moving in to help with the kids. We were in a bigger house, spending less money, and had assistance with the kids. We could always get another home later.

Christy going to school was a big event in our lives. Any time your firstborn goes to school it is a happy and yet sad occasion. They are going into a new world and are no longer your little baby. A favorite story about her first day was when she got to her class. The teacher had put on the wall outside the classroom all the children's names in that room. Not knowing she went by her middle name, "Marlena" was on the wall. Christy searched the wall, and when she didn't see Christy, she looked up at us and said, "I don't have to go."

Christy was our best student of the three, and no doubt Craig was the greatest challenge. Their mother was always volunteering whatever she could do for the kids' classrooms when they were in grade school. If something needed to be done or a project needed help, she would always be there. The children could not have asked for a better mother during these years.

Our time with the children has always been special to us. Their mother took pictures of everything, and they all have photo albums of their youth. I can only imagine how many discs we would have if digital cameras had been around. There are few things I enjoy more than looking at the children's pictures. From baby pictures to graduation, she was there to capture the moment, and we should always be grateful. You will never meet anyone who got a bigger kick out of taking and showing off the pictures of their family, and she is still that way today. Saying she was proud of her three children just doesn't begin to describe how she felt. There wasn't anything she wouldn't do for them. The children were always her first priority, and at times this was difficult because of the time it took away from us just being together as a couple. All married couples deal with this from time to time.

We never got to go on many vacations when they were young because of funds and things they were doing. All of the kids were active in all the activities a school can offer, so there was somewhere to be every day. Renee played softball and was in gymnastics. Christy was going to church activities, and later Craig was playing some kind of ball year-round. Our lives were full of activities, but because of our finances, this entire time was difficult. I worked two jobs many times to make ends meet so that she didn't have to get a second job. Her time to be with the kids was so important that I never wanted that to be jeopardized. When the money was coming in from whatever I was doing, times would be terrific, but if we struggled, it was uncomfortable. It sounds as if she was all about money, and that is not true. She just wanted a stable and reliable income that I very rarely provided.

When the girls went to junior high, things became even more hectic. Choir was a big part of our family, and both Christy and Renee are talented singers. The choir director for the school system was Janis Dawson, who taught us both. Their mother became a choir fanatic; there was not an office in the parent organization that she didn't hold at some time. Janis could call on her to do anything knowing it would get accomplished on time and right. Very few people call Janis anything but Janis or Ms. Dawson, but I've always called her J. D., which I assure you is a term of endearment. Parents could go on choir trips with the students as sponsors if they worked enough hours in the organization, and she never once missed a trip. They went to New York, Florida, San Antonio, Colorado, California, and Canada and won every place they sang. So although as a family we didn't travel as much as we should have, the girls and later Craig would take great trips with their mother. I never went for several reasons, but the most important was I wanted her to have fun with the kids and enjoy her time away so when she came back she would miss me.

Craig began to play soccer when he was four, but it wasn't his game—too much running. At the age of seven, he started baseball and basketball. Baseball has been not only his best sport but something at the age of twenty-four he still plays competitively. When we went to sign him up that first year, the high school head baseball coach, Paul McCracken, was trying to get the Little League up and running. Since he knew I not only graduated from there but played on the baseball team, he asked if I could help. I became the league president and oversaw the organization for the next six years. What their mother did for the choir I did for the baseball league. The first year I coached Craig's team plus a twelve-year-old group. There was not a night that first year, except Wednesdays, that I was not at the ballpark for one team or the other or for some league reason. For the next six years, it would be like that. Also, because Craig loved to play and was a pitcher, he got picked up most weekends to play.

The hardest part of this time was being able to do for the children and still make sure everything was taken care of financially. There is no way to tell you or my children how sad I feel that I didn't do better for them and their mother. Most men will look back and say they could have done better, and sometimes it is true. In my case, there is no room for doubt. Whether my former wife ever loved me or not is a question we will discuss later; the fact is it would have been easier for her to if during this time I had been more success-ful. It was not that we were dirt poor or that we went hungry. It was just that sometimes we had to decide between something for the kids or paying the electric bill. If it came down to a choice between something fun for the kids or paying bills, I chose fun. I realized later in life that this trait caused us unnecessary hardships.

Going from event to event was great because we spent time together as a family. Everyone always went to see what the other was doing unless things overlapped. When we were all together, it was always one of the best parts of our marriage. Children should never be a reason that a family stays together, and I never thought that was true with us till in the end when for her she said that was the case. At the time, you would never have guessed we had any problems because we always did things together as a family and as a couple. If we were not together, it was because one parent was with one kid and the other was watching someone else.

When the girls got to junior high, we moved to another rent house and Mary moved out. It was a neat home with a sunken living room and a big yard. It was right down the street from where she worked and still in the school district. We lived there for two years then moved back out to the addition that was closer to the schools. The high school, junior high, and grade school were all within walking distance and right next to each other. Although most of my family thinks I'm crazy, I still have ties to the school and help raise money and public awareness for school projects.

In the late eighties, I tried to go back to school to gain the education we thought I needed to get a better-paying sales opportunity. Attending school late in life is difficult with the pressure of making a living, going to your children's activities, and spending quality time with your wife. I went to work on a loading dock at night and went to school in the morning. Most of the people who attended class there were quite a bit younger than me to say the least. School was enjoyable and challenging all at the same time, but it made it hard to again pay the bills because we had no real reserve funds, and if anything went wrong or came up unexpectedly, we had problems. After a year and half, I left to find a better paying job and never went back.

While the kids were in school, these were the jobs I had: the furniture store; a finance company; sold cars, portable buildings, spas, patio furniture, insurance; a traveling closer; and the loading dock. There are probably more I have forgotten. Some I worked at for several years, so it was not that I was changing all the time, but if there was what I thought was better opportunity or if it made it more convenient to be with the kids, I made the move. Some of the jobs were salary, and some were not, but I never did well enough either way to put us where we should have been. The children have never said that they felt deprived or that their lives were any less than what they should have been, but I know that is not true.

Christy's senior year we finally bought another home. It was an older home right around the corner from my parents. It had a big add-on that made it a four-bedroom house with a large covered patio. Both of the girls could finally have their own room, and we owned instead of renting. The house had problems, to say the least, and thirteen years later I'm still getting them fixed. I have decided that homes are nothing more than a continued remodeling project.

Our house was a great sense of joy and conflict in our marriage. We were always fixing something, and there was never enough money to either do it right or the way she wanted it done. I hate to paint. There is no way to tell you how much I hate to paint, but she was not only good at it but she knew how she wanted it done. There was only one way to do or fix anything, and that was the way she wanted it done, so we just let her do it. She always enjoyed remodeling or painting the house, but the fact that I didn't like to help always annoyed her. She would be more upset when I didn't meet her standards and usually did it over anyway.

The neighborhood that we moved into was the same one she and I grew up in. Both our parents lived within walking distance. The area looks just the same as it did when we were kids; only the people changed. It is a lower-middle-class area with young and old neighbors. When we moved, it was the right house for us, but as the kids grew and left, she felt we should have lived in a nicer part of town in a better home. We were only about six years away from having the home paid for, so it made no sense to me to move and start all over at our age, but she never saw it that way. Our living room, den, bathroom, and kitchen had all been remodeled. The covered patio was fourteen-by-thirty-two feet and great for parties, so it was and is a nice home with good neighbors—just not good enough for her. Christy graduated in '96.

Renee was a sophomore, and Craig started junior high, but things never did slow down. Renee was cheerleading and involved in choir and several other school groups, and Craig was still playing ball. Their mother went to all the games but to this day doesn't know the first thing about football, baseball, or basketball. Whether a game has an inning a period or a quarter was not important to her only that her children were either playing or cheering. I coached both Renee and Craig in the sports they played, and some say I was too hard on both of them; there is some truth in that, especially with the boy.

However, one of the favorite stories Renee likes to tell is how mean her dad was to her. She was ten playing softball, and I was coaching. At a crucial point in a game, I called time out and brought all the infielders in to go over strategy since she was the catcher she had on her mask. The play was going to be at home, and she needed to catch the ball, so to emphasize the point, I grabbed her facemask, pulled her up close, and said, "Catch the ball!" Now I would never recommend that now, but I wanted to make my point. She never played after that year again. In reality, she was too small to play much longer, but it was wrong on my part, and her mother was not a happy camper over it because she felt I embarrassed Renee, and she was right.

As much as I could write series of short stories about Renee and her exploits, Craig's sports stories and school life would almost be a book. His mother thought from the very beginning I was way too hard on him in many ways but mostly when it came to sports. Craig was not only good at most things he did; he understood the games early on and liked being coached. In our house, we always played to win, and no one ever let anyone win because of age or any other reason. Renee, Craig, and I all hate to lose. Christy and their mom just played to play the game. I taught him how to play with respect to the games and to play the right way. He practiced a great deal and became a better-than-average player in the sports he played, but when he could do things better, I was there to point them out. I just didn't always do it the way it should have been done. He always understood it was for his own good, and what went on between the lines ended when the game was over. I never once loved him any less because of his performance, but his mother felt at times I stepped over the line, and there is truth in that. I just don't think it ever affected our relationship. I hope I'm right.

After Renee graduated in '98, she went off to college. Christy was working and living out on her own, so we didn't see as much of them. Parents in many ways may be glad when the children leave, but they want them to come and visit as much as possible. Motherhood is a difficult job, and it never ends no matter how old a child becomes, and with both girls gone and not stopping by, it was a difficult transition for us both. We would have four more years with Craig in high school to keep us busy. Four years seems like a long time, but I looked up, and he was playing in his last high school baseball game, and it was over. In many ways, so was the marriage for her.

THE BEDROOM

This is a delicate chapter to write since both of our parents and children are still with us; it's not going to be about specifics but more about attitudes. From our honeymoon till New Year's Day 2009, the last time we were together, not much changed with us in the bedroom. Making love was never a key element in our marriage. We both had very different ideas on what role this should and would play in our relationship. It was not that we didn't enjoy being together; it was that we viewed love-making and the things around it differently. After we separated, she told me that the only reason she thought I was married to her was for the sex. There may not be a crueler or more hurtful thing someone can say to someone else.

I have been a very affectionate person all my life. I love to hold and kiss and be with whomever I'm with at the time. When I got married, I wanted to be with her as much as possible as any newlywed husband would. In the beginning, this was great because we were each other's first intimate encounter. We were no different from other couples in that this was not only all new but at times awkward. Even though we may not have been head over in heels in love, we still enjoyed the intimacy of being with someone and making them happy. As we became more at ease with each other, it was even more pleasurable.

Many factors came into play as we grew older that would affect how often we would be together. At first it was the children, then stress, then finances, and lastly, a lack of desire on her part. During our thirty-three years, I can honestly say I never made her be with me if she either didn't feel good, was not in the mood, or for any other reason. As the years passed, she found more and more excuses for us not to be together. She has never been totally comfortable about the subject; we never talked about it in or out of the bed. Not that sex was taboo; it was just something that was never discussed or joked about. To this day she has no sense of humor when it comes to sex.

I would have been with her any time and any place; she was not that spontaneous. It had to be just the right place and time, especially in the middle part of the marriage. Surprisingly, the end was much like the beginning, except I think she was trying to find what she hadn't found before and to keep me happy to a degree. After Craig moved out and in between people moving back, our time together was very good. We went on several great vacations to San Diego, Santa Fe, Las Vegas, Shreveport, and Montana. While on vacation, she would let her hair and guard down, relax, and become the woman and partner I always wanted. When she was in the mood to be together, she was a very sexy woman. These times are wonderful memories for me because she truly seemed to be in love with me.

She always felt that any attention I showed her was simply to get her in to bed. No matter how many times I tried to explain that was not the case, she took it that way. If I walked up behind her and put my arms around her and kissed the back of her neck lovingly, she thought it had some sexual overtones. It was almost impossible to give her a real, passionate kiss unless we were about to make love. One of her complaints was that we never just held hands or cuddled without taking it further; most married men hear this at some point. The difference with us was that when she would be affectionate with me, it was one of her signs she was in the mood—not always but a great deal of the time. At the end, there were times that neither one of us took the time to love each other or meet the other one's needs.

I'm not sure if this happens in all marriages, but when she wanted to get pregnant, it would change her completely. For eight to ten weeks or till we found out she was having a baby would be our most active time together. It wouldn't matter what was going on. All she knew was that she wanted to be pregnant, and there was only one way for that to happen. While this was a great time for me, it had a down side because as soon as she knew, the party stopped. It seemed weird at the time and still puzzles me to this day how one minute she was a ball of fire and the next shut down on a dime.

Throughout the marriage, I always tried to please her as much as possible. It was important to me that she enjoyed our time together—partly because I felt the more she did, the more she would want to be together. Unfortunately, that never became the case. It can be difficult for a spouse when the marriage is over not to wonder if they were unable to fulfill the other's needs, or was there something different they were looking for. When I asked her about this, she replied that our sex together had not been the problem but that since she wasn't in love with me, it was difficult to always want to be with me. All men and woman have urges that may eventually override their feelings or feel an obligation to their partner. She would at times drop little hints that let me know she wanted to be intimate, and those times were special.

Again this is not a chapter about sordid details. We have three beautiful children that would not have been born had we not been together. I felt that making love was an integral part of marriage; she felt it was at times for pleasure and mostly an obligation. It was both frustrating and bewildering at times that someone who proclaimed to love me didn't want to be with me. Many nights it was like a cat-and-mouse game. It seldom came naturally. It was, until the end, the second biggest conflict in our marriage next to finances. The saddest part of it all was that when we were together and she would look me in the eyes and say "I love you," I always believed her.

HER

It would seem easy to describe someone you have lived with for thirty-three years, but if I knew her that well, perhaps we wouldn't be here today. I have stated many times that she is an attractive woman who I have always wanted to be with. Even before we were married, I spent a great deal of my spare time with her and have always considered her my best friend. People often can be one way around everyone else and then become different with the people they are closest. When others got to know her over a long period of time, they would see certain personality traits that at first might have been missed, but others would be there from the beginning.

I talked about her work ethic earlier; she is a motivated individual who only knows one way to do things: the way she thinks they should be done. Not that she is wrong about how things should be accomplished; very often she just thinks she has the best plan or solution. Ask her to do anything and I promise it will get accomplished on time and in a way you would be proud. There has never been a project she was asked to do that she could not finish. This is true in her job, school groups, or any other field. She is organized and efficient in all things she takes on. At home, our house was as well kept a home as you could find anywhere. Her decorating skills, although not always to my taste, were excellent. Our home was a place you could be proud of, and most of that was due to her ability to decorate and maintain the home. Sounds like the perfect wife.

Her mom and dad divorced when she was thirteen, and she was left in charge of two younger brothers and a younger sister. Going to work at that age is no fun for anyone, but add the responsibility of watching younger siblings and that makes it tough. She missed out on many school functions because she either had to work or watch everyone. I think she has always resented the fact that this burden was placed on her at such a young age. And when she felt I didn't relieve that burden but simply transferred it to me, that resentment grew through the years. Quitting work has been her primary goal for years. She wanted me to find something that would allow her to stay home and just be a mom. None of the people we knew could do this, and if they did, they were worse off than we were. However, that was her greatest wish. I never understood why she thought it was some divine right that this should have happened to her and never came to pass with me. The story of her hard teen life has been told many times to our children to the point they are immune.

Having faith and trust in people is something she has very little of. She is distrustful of others and suspicious of their actions, seeing only the worst in most people or being critical of their motives. Her view of life never allowed her to become the type of person who believed in anyone or anything. Completely independent, she has always depended on herself and her abilities. She can be headstrong to the point of not being able to see any position but her own, and once her mind is made up, no facts or other information will change her point of view.

It is difficult to be critical of someone that you still care for a great deal, especially when they have so many traits you love. No one is perfect in any marriage; we all have our own faults. Let me tell all the things I have admired and loved about her for years. It may seem strange that I would still think of her in a positive way, but she is still my favorite person.

In the bedroom chapter, I didn't want to go into specifics, but here I will say that she has the best lips I ever kissed. Kissing her was something I wanted to do and would do anytime. I have very small hands, and hers fit mine in every way. Being Hispanic gave her skin a tan tone most of the year, and in certain clothes she was incredible to admire. Many times I simply watched her dress and thought about her beauty. When we went to a function that required dressing up, she always looked amazing. To say I didn't think about her would be a great understatement for I thought about her all the time. When she did touch the back of my neck or held my arm, I got chills all over. To this day I know exactly how she felt and tasted.

She has a smile that would bring me the greatest joy. Her laugh was a laugh that was genuine and honest. There was never a soul who asked for her help that she didn't lend a hand or whatever was needed. Many times in our marriage it would be her fortitude that carried us through. There is no way to tell how much I enjoyed holding her and being with her; we seemed to fit each other so well. I felt everything would be fine and work out when I held her close. She has always had a calming effect on me and does so to this day. No matter how bad things got for me before, now she is the only one who just by talking to me can calm me down.

Being a mother to our children was her greatest joy. I said before when the children were young she was the best mom anyone could want. That never changed. It was just as the kids grew older they saw a different side to their mother. Her personality is out-going and friendly, the kind most people are drawn to. She dresses with class and taste with a limited bud-get then and now. Making hot sauce and cooking are talents she developed over the years. The pound cake and brownies she made were the best. There is noth-ing she wasn't good at when she set her mind to it.

I don't want to paint her as a terrible person because she's not. We had a long marriage that I was happy in for the most part. She never abused me or treated me horribly; she had trouble treating me as a wife should treat her husband. If I made a decision that to her seemed arbitrary, it would set her off. She wanted me to be the foundation of the family but never wanted to really put me in charge. We had sort of a 50/50 mar-riage. I'll talk about it later, but she had a hard time letting go of control. Everyone has personality traits that may at times rub people the wrong way. Our family's problem was that we never confronted her with the things that she did to us and other people.

Honesty and straightforwardness are great assets, but they must be tempered with tact and understanding. Many times her lack of either would raise eyebrows or bring a strange look from some third party. It was never that she meant to give you the impression you were clueless; it just came across sounding that way. The tone of her voice could have that condescending sound. If you asked her a question she thought you should know, the tone became even coarser. If your opinion was different from hers, she had the knack of irritating you with looks and voice tone. Having the ability to think about what you're going to say before you say it was never in her gene pool. She would say the most outrageous things to people and never think she said anything wrong. In our house, we call that "mom being mom."

The other saying was that "if something is green and mom says it is blue, remember green has blue in it." Meaning, she is never wrong. Living with someone who can do anything better than you, is never wrong and doesn't say "I'm sorry" even if it would persuade St. Peter to open the Pearly Gates, can wear on a person and a family. I could count on one hand the number of times in our marriage she said she was sorry. There was nothing she hated more than being proven wrong unless it had to admit it. If she was wrong, she had an excuse or it was someone else's fault.

For some reason, she always felt it was her responsibility to correct anyone who misspoke about anything. Misstate a store name, restaurant, a place or event, and right away you would be corrected. It made no difference if you were family or friend, young or old. She informed you of the correct information. But with me she took it to a higher level. Whether it was just us in the car or in a crowd of people, she would pounce on the correction as if it was her civic duty. For a time, I would get two home building store names mixed up; one of them was closed, so she knew which I was talking about yet would correct me every time. With the correction came that condescending tone of "you can't be that stupid." People often said I *over-married*. I always hated that because who are they to judge, and what do they know about my life with her? The worst part for me was that she, in the beginning, never took up for me, and only after I mentioned it did she do so halfheartedly.

Showing her emotions was something that never came easy to her, with me or the kids. Not to say she didn't tell them she loved them or hold and kiss them. It was that she didn't do it all the time. It was so seldom that she told me she loved me before I told her first that when it did happen, it was as special as it got for me. After we remodeled our kitchen in 2008, we were standing by the sink, and she came up to me, put her arms around me, gave a sweet kiss, and said, "I really do love you." It may be my favorite memory about our time together; yet she says she never remembers doing it, and that broke my heart. To this day, if I say "I love you" to our children, they always answer, "I love my dad." Affection was something that she struggled with throughout the marriage, maybe because in her own life it was never shown to her by her family. I'm not sure. Today she tries to be more loving with the children, yet it is difficult for them because it wasn't always there in their youth. The love she has for our kids has been a mother's love and is so today. With me it simply depended on the time and place of our marriage. If things were going well, she was wonderful and affectionate, but if we were having money problems, it was almost nonexistent.

She could be the sweetest person you would meet, but many times, especially later on, she just wasn't nice and was oblivious to other's feelings. She always hoped I would be more successful. I always hoped she would become the considerate and thoughtful person she was capable of being. Now the world revolves solely around her, and what is important to her first and her perspective is the only right perspective.

I want to end this chapter saying that whatever faults she has, it never changed my true devotion or love for her. She will continue to be my favorite person, and I fear I will always wish I was her husband.

ME

First, I'm a wreck! Trying to be honest and objective about oneself can be difficult and painful. What was it about me that she either never loved or now finds unattractive? What could I have done better or differently to have avoided this situation? Many things have been talked about already that I wish I had done better for my former wife and children. We all have shortcomings, and I am no different, so I'll tell you about me and try not to do it through rose-colored glasses.

Many of my faults are universal to both men and women and may not seem to be reasons for a divorce. While that may be true that if you look at each one individually, they must be taken as a whole because the sum of these faults was part of what affected her feelings about me

Do I talk about the good things first or speak of my many faults? The faults may take longer, so I believe we will start there. It is my prayer every day now that I become the kind of person who not only God would want me to be but that I want to become. My greatest fault I believe is that we didn't include God and faith in our marriage. Not that faith can save a marriage, but it gives you something to lean on and fall back on in times of strife and discontent. I was married in a church by a pastor in front of God and took those vows to heart. Our religious differences should not have kept us from finding a faith that was right for us and showing that faith to God.

We never prayed together until an event that happened to Renee, which I will discuss later. By this time, I had gotten the news and was struggling with all the events in my life. At the church I have attended, announcements include the anniversaries of the couples who go there, and it is obvious that some of these are not their first marriages. So faith is not a guarantee that a marriage will work, but what could it hurt? I read in one of the many books people have given me that couples should have the same faith; there is merit in that. What may be more important is that you take the time to pray and worship in some way. I pray that God will watch over and bless her each day, but I should have prayed with her that He watch over and guide us.

The second great fault is not listening to what my wife was saying to me about her concerns with our lives, the marriage, and her happiness. We had talked on more than one occasion about the state of our marriage after Craig left, but either I heard what I wanted to hear or simply ignored her. Communication, they say, is a cornerstone to a successful marriage. When we talked many times, each wanted their point of view to be the right one and never considered things from the other's perspective. She felt that when we talked, I spoke to her like a salesman trying to pitch my side.

Perhaps that is true, but it was never intended. My voice has a tendency to get loud even when I try to talk low and especially when I get excited or in heated discussions. This was something that drove her crazy. All discussions needed to be done in a calm and monotone voice and never in a public place. I can be under control with my emotions with everything I do now, including golf (which was not always my history), but with her, my emotions run high, and that has never been easy to do.

When I was young, one of the personality traits I was known for was my temper. It was not a violent temper, just one that got loud and sometimes physical with whatever object I could get my hands on.

One of my former wife's stories about my temper was from before we were married. I lost at a poker game, picked up a glass mug, went outside, and threw it into the side of a building and went nuts. During the separation, through the divorce, and since, I have more than once let my emotions trigger my temper. No matter what I try, I can't seem to just walk away. I have said some things that in the heat of the moment were not true and I could never mean, but my temper got the best of me, and I know I hurt her deeply. Any time I feel that I have in some way hurt her, it nearly drives me insane with guilt. Counting the number of times in the last nine months I've said I was sorry would only bring me embarrassment. My children have seen me angry, but my temper never came into play with them. Only Craig saw it once with a lawnmower that wouldn't start that I destroyed and when he got between us when I was very upset with her several years back. Although I always controlled my temper, she thought it would pop up at times. She was never afraid of me and knew I would never hurt her in any way. It just worried her that it was there.

My next fault may be difficult to explain . However, I believe it is something that has affected my life and marriage. Not living up to one's potential is a sad realization. When Craig played ball, we would sometimes talk about players who wasted their talent. Either they never did the things that were necessary to be the best they could be or they did something stupid that cost them the opportunity. The latter was never the case for me, but the first was certainly true. I tried to find success in many fields, but seldom did I become the best I could have been. In several careers, I was good at my job, such as the job I have now as a traveling closer. I was talented, but they were never going to give us the lifestyle she and I wanted. I said once before that when you are good at something, it makes you overlook all of the negatives. She had always wanted me to have a steady job and a regular paycheck. What I have been doing for the last six years was one of the few times it happened, and even then my paycheck varied from week to week, making it hard to budget. I'm not sure what I could have become if I had found the right opportunity. I've never been sure I have ever done what I was either destined to do or where my true talent lay.

Many times I would put the things I wanted to do ahead of our family and budget responsibilities. At the beginning of our marriage and up until a short time ago, if I thought it was important or just something I wanted to do, I would do it whether we could afford to or not. I'm not sure that this was selfish as much as it was irresponsible. What I do know is that it was inexcusable. There were times I would take money to play softball early in the marriage and golf later on that could have been better used for the family or to do something with her instead. We never had the electricity turned off or went hungry because of my actions; still, it caused more than one disagreement and hard feelings between us. As I look back, it was something that if I had the ability or desire to think through, I could have seen how this upset her.

Age gives one a different view on life and situations. As I grew older, I realized things could be seen from a different perspective depending on one's perception. When I was younger, I was known to be a very opinionated individual. Rarely did I think I was wrong or that another might be right. I looked at things almost always in black and white with no room for gray. With many people, that view of me never changed even though I did. Not that I don't believe strongly about issues; it's just that I have learned there are two sides to every story. As I grew older and matured, I learned that if I listened and looked at things from all points of view, a solution would appear. So many mistakes in our marriage could have been avoided if I had learned this earlier.

If I had one personality trait or fault that I wish I had never developed and one that nearly drove my former wife insane, it would be procrastination. This is something that unfortunately I passed down to Christy and Craig. Where she was one to get things done right then, I would wait to do them when I felt like it or on my time table. I can't begin to tell you how many times she asked me to do something that could have been done right then and it would take me days to finish. Where she is a perfectionist, I would do just whatever it took to do the job without worrying if it looked professional. Having to ask me to do something several times seems now just inconsiderate. Manual labor was never something I enjoyed doing, and home repairs were way down on my list of things I enjoyed. I was never good at doing these things, and it frustrated me when I didn't do them well or up to her standards.

Playing golf is not necessarily a fault. However, placing an importance of it above all else is wrong. I played golf for years on Sunday afternoon with a group of brothers regardless of what else was going on in our lives. I never understood why she objected to me playing, except when we couldn't afford it, until I realized she felt it was more important for me to be there than to be with her. Nothing was more important to me than her, but because I made such an issue out of playing or acted childish when I didn't get to play, she felt it made our relationship secondary.

With many marriages, husbands and wives have outside hobbies and interests. These activities take time away from being together. Some couples adjust and accept this behavior as part of the marriage and the person. Husbands can go on hunting and fishing trips for weeks while wives spend weekends shopping to their heart's content. Our marriage never had that luxury because of my dedication to play golf and her lack of a desire to develop other interests besides her children and school activities.

We both could never understand why the other felt the way they did about what they did or appreciated the time we spent doing things together. If I spent twenty dollars on golf, she felt she was entitled to the same amount of spending money whether we did something else together or not. Going to the dollar movie after I spent substantially more than that playing golf was something she never understood. Perhaps she was right, but I never thought the price of the activity was as important as doing it together. If golf, bowling, or antique shopping is something one enjoys, remember in some way to include your spouse and, when possible, it is important to ensure time and resources are equal.

Golf became the lightning rod for all things in our marriage she was unhappy about, and many times when I should have done things with her, I chose golf. It may seem simple to say, but if on certain occasions or just every once in a while I had chosen to be with her instead, we might still be together today.

Whatever my redeeming personal traits are is not for me to say. People have formed their opinions about me, and to try and justify my character, personality, and life would only be self-serving. What I will say is that I feel I have always been a loving and caring father to my children. I can't think of many people in my life that didn't like or enjoy my company. I always treat people the way I would want to be treated, and I'm a nice person who thinks of others. I always wanted the best for her and for her to be happy. There was never a day in my marriage that I didn't kiss my wife, say I love you, and tell her how pretty she looked. She was everything to me, and it is tragic that she didn't feel she was the most important part of my life or that I didn't love her above everything else because that was always true. As a husband and a provider, I may not have done for her as well as I should have, but I always loved her more than I could say and thought that was the most important part of a marriage.

FIFTY-FIFTY

I don't know if other marriages set up this way, but because we both worked, she felt that responsibilities should be split evenly. Not that there was anything wrong with that philosophy, and for the most part I agreed. It still made for some interesting decisions. We never lived by the unspoken rule that the man had the only say and final word in any matter. Chores were divided up generally along traditional boundaries but not always. She never once mowed the yard or dug up a tree stump. I never cleaned the bathroom unless it was absolutely necessary.

Cooking was split between us; when one of us cooked, it was the other one's responsibility to clean up. So whenever I could, I made dinner! We were both good cooks, but each of us had foods that we were better at preparing. Our children were extremely picky eaters when they were small, and because we were always on the go, we didn't eat a lot of what you would call healthy meals. We even had what we called bum night, meaning whatever you could find and fix, you could eat. Whoever got to the good leftovers first was a happy camper. We both did laundry; though, I'm sure she would say she did the majority. Housekeeping was primarily her job simply so it could be done the way she wanted.

Depending on if I was employed at the time or if my schedule allowed, I was expected to do more around the house, and that was fair. I never minded doing more if that was the case, except she never really appreciated that I did or it wasn't good enough for her. Whether it was me or the children, whatever we cleaned or took care of, there was another way she would have done it or she would simply do it over to her satisfaction. It got to the point that the children would only do things halfheartedly because they knew she would come in behind them and do it right. With all of us doing things on her schedule was difficult because she wanted things done right then, and, except for Renee, occasionally that was a problem.

I've talked to other married men and couples, along with single women I know, and many seem to be surprised that I helped out as much as I did. Some men said they never cooked, did laundry, and hadn't vacuumed in their lives. Women said their husbands almost never did anything around the house if it wasn't considered a man's chore. If they did cook, it was on the grill, and they never cleaned up! Well, I am sure this is not true with all husbands, but it is with a great many. I just wish she had appreciated what I did. I did them because I wanted to, not because I had to. I'm not trying to paint myself as a perfect husband in this area but just someone who did these things because I felt it was the right thing.

In our marriage, along with the 50/50 rule, we had way too much *mine* and *yours* and not enough *ours*. I can't tell you how many times the house was referred to as her home. When we got married, she had complete china and cookware sets that she had purchased, and I was reminded more than once it was hers. If she bought something, it was never as if she was getting it for us as a couple but more along the lines of who it was for. She once bought a bed set that suddenly became her bed set. If she picked out and bought the vacuum cleaner, it was her vacuum cleaner. Except for my Beatles collection, I don't think there was anything I claimed as mine. I had through the years collected a large collection of Beatles items such as posters, books, figurines, and special pictures Christy had made for me, of which I'm very proud. But with her, it seemed that many items and possessions were thought of along whom they belonged to.

How it came to be like that I'm not really sure except because she is so independent and worried about her well-being. I would at times be annoyed with her attitude about this, and it was discussed more than once; however, she never changed her thinking. Couples should share not only what they own but think of it as a gift that they have someone to enjoy them with. The owner of a particular thing is not important; sharing them together is very important. . If many years ago I had taken a strong stance about this, perhaps I could have changed her way of thinking. During the divorce, it became an issue on several levels. Things she felt were hers, the kids and

I felt no longer belonged to her because she left the marriage. The children contended to a degree that "if you go, you can't take anything," but I didn't let that happen and I discuss that later.

Someone always has to have the last say in most decisions. That was difficult with us because everything had to be 50/50. If I did make a decision without discussing it with her, she felt I was acting like a general in the family. When we did talk about finances, the children, or any other matter, our points of view would lead to different solutions most of the time. What should the solution be? We never took turns or anything like that, but some compromise would have to be struck. Not that compromise is bad in any marriage, and there is always that in a marriage. It is how the couples accept that compromise. She was never good at accepting any point of view other than her own.

Many times I knew my solution was a better way or answer to our problem, but in order to keep the peace, I would give in and appease her. Appeasement can be a solution as well as a point of conflict if not handled well; my negotiating skills usually kept the peace. Married couples who never learn to compromise and which battle is worth the fight might not last as long as we did. If you live in one of those rare homes where one party makes all the decisions, I'm not sure what your chances are.

There were many things that one party decided, however, in our home. Paint was a big one for her; I never once picked out the color of paint that she was going to be put on the wall! Anything that had to do with the kitchen was pretty much her domain. Decorating the house was left up to her taste, except for the Beatle room. What she picked here was not always what I liked, but I wanted her to be happy. When she left, I repainted and decorated to my taste.

When it came to cars, lawnmowers, TVs, and such, I usually got the last word. There would be input from her, but I made the decision. This may seem strange. I'm not sure how other couples handle these types of issues. For many years, this worked for us because we knew the boundaries. If there was an area of gray, again some compromise would be met. A college professor once told me that in all things there is a tradeoff. I always tried to live by three rules: treat others the way you want to be treated, what goes around comes around, and there is a tradeoff for everything. When I grew older, I added a fourth: there are always two sides to a story.

The biggest area that we had the most disagreement was, of course, finances. To this day we are still bound together because of our financial situation, much to her dismay. What to pay, who to pay, how much to pay, and when to pay were questions that were asked most paydays. Now since she was a bookkeeper, it made sense that she would keep the checkbook and pay the bills. I would occasionally make a suggestion, but she generally knew what needed to be paid and in what order. The problem that arose more times than not was that there wasn't enough to take care of everyone, which I have stated more than once was mostly my fault.

At the very end right before I got the news, I began to take a more active role and right before she left, complete control. Somewhere along the way our philosophies had made a change to where I was more of the one who wanted to figure a way out of our situation and was trying to take steps to see that happen. Since she had been in control for so long, it was an adjustment that was hard for her to make, so paying the bills was a tense and stressful event. We have made progress in this area but would have been further along had she stayed. When we divorced, we split the credit cards that were in her name 50/50.

Another great mistake in our marriage is that we didn't really share our goals with each other. In many ways there were no goals at all, just living as best as we could from paycheck to paycheck. Goals are more than money. Couples need to have a vision of where they want to be not only financially but personally in their relationship and spiritually. We never sat down and listed the things we wanted to accomplish or do together. I don't know if we were not on the same page or different pages altogether.

There was never a unity toward the things we wanted to accomplish but more of a confused state of self-objectives. In most of the books I have read, it seems that financial security is a strong priority for women, and I never really provided that for her. Unfortunately, now that she is gone I have done better with the two jobs and perhaps could have done that, but I don't know if it would matter if she didn't love me.

CHRISTMAS

It may seem weird to write about Christmas in a book about divorce, but believe me, it was a large problem in our marriage. Now my family loves Christmas, and the inside of our home and our children's homes were decorated to the hilt. We had as many as four Christmas trees in the house some years with decorations everywhere. We have cabinets and closets full of decorations of all shape, sizes, and themes. Our decorations started going up at least by Thanksgiving weekend and stayed till New Year's Day.

The first Christmas of our marriage we went and cut down a tree on our own. We lived in an apartment that had a normal ceiling, and this tree was not even close to standing straight up. They always seem to look smaller in the great outdoors. So we cut and trimmed until it fit. It was a lot of fun but trying at the same time because doing things like that together even in the beginning was hard. She always decorated the tree. We would have themes most years and not all of them Christmas-y. They always looked exceptional just not traditional.

Our Christmas in the beginning went like this: Christmas Eve night we went to my parents until around ten and then over to her dad's to go to mid-night Mass, back to his house for dinner, and opened presents at two in the morning. Then we got up in the morning to go to my grandma and grandpa Baker's, over to grandmother and granddad Carr's, and to see her mother somewhere in the mix. We were usually exhausted by the time it was all over, but we loved every minute. After Christy was born, we had to add Christmas Santa time as well early in the morning for her and later for the other two. In time, we stopped having Christmas at her dad's after midnight Mass because it was just too hard on all the grandchildren.

Midnight Mass at Christmas was one of my favorite things with her family. Being raised Baptist, I had never seen the beautiful service of a midnight Mass during the season. No matter what faith you believe, everyone should witness this as many times as you can to help put Christmas in the right place in one's heart. Her dad took great joy in all of us going to the service, and he has always been someone I have admired and enjoyed seeing happy. She had five stepbrothers and stepsisters by the time we got married, so it was a large gathering at the home along with her brothers and sisters. When it came time to pass out the presents, unlike at my home where it was done in a neat and orderly fashion, they just started throwing them to each other and opening them as fast as they could. It was like a semi-controlled tornado but a blast to see and be around. I promise my first few Christmases there are some of my most precious memories.

In the beginning and for several years we always had a real Christmas tree. Some years we went and cut one down or went to the local school or Boy Scout lot to get one. I not only enjoyed having a real tree, but getting out and finding just the right tree (or in some cases the wrong tree) is a great part of the season. In a way, it is sad that children only pull a tree out of a box today. A real tree is all I had ever known, but later when her allergies got worse, we bought an artificial tree and added more through the years. I understood it was best for her and the children but always missed the smell and look of a real tree. Christmas was her domain.

We laugh sometimes about the meticulous way she would decorate the tree. Every ball and light had to be just perfectly aligned and balanced. There could never be a bulb out of place. When the kids helped her, she would let them decorate the way they wanted; then as soon as they were in bed or gone, she'd redecorate. They eventually caught on and just stopped helping, and I never even got in the way and only assisted when asked because it avoided confusion. Being a perfectionist can be a good thing at times, but when it is something like your family decorating the tree, perhaps it isn't necessary.

Each year brought new decorations for the tree and some years' themes. There were theme trees such as snowmen, Santa, angels, wooden ornaments, glass ornaments, and others such as the Hawaiian and lavender trees to name a few. Now again these always looked exceptional. Her ability to decorate anything was never a question. It was just that there was very little if any input from me about what I wanted and liked. The last few years when we had several trees she would decorate one of the small ones they way she knew I would like and had been brought up with, but that was her way of appeasing me.

Putting up outside Christmas lights one year became a big thing. When I didn't put them up in the time frame she wanted to and was less than enthusiastic about doing it at all, it became an issue. I've said before that many times I was inconsiderate when it came to doing things that she asked me to do, but part of that was if we did them together someone was going to be unhappy. The lights did go up, but she did most of the work, and each year for several years after she would put them up again.

Of course the biggest problem most years was the purchasing of gifts. The obvious thing was that it might center on money, which is not the whole story. Although there were years that it was difficult to buy for the children and family, we almost always figured a way. Our children, I believe, would say they had great Christmases their whole lives and never felt deprived. Still it would have been nice to do more for them at times. The real issue was over who and when the gifts were bought.

Many years I never bought one single gift for my children, or later, my grandsons. She began buying Christmas in August, and it was done by the day after Thanksgiving. The problem with that was that I seldom got asked to go on these shopping excursions. Christmas shopping, I contended, should be done during the season. Sure, you get great buys in August, but where is the fun in if you're not doing it to "Silver Bells." Her point was about the savings, not the joy of going together. Our next to last Christmas I said that that year nothing could be bought without me being there, and unless it was absolutely necessary, nothing was to be bought until after Thanksgiving. We went together and bought almost everything together as a couple. It's another great memory for me. The next year and our last together things went back to the way it was before. I found out all of what had been bought either when it was being wrapped or on Christmas day.

As our children got older, it was beginning to become difficult to work out a time that we as a family could be together. Christmas Eve as the children grew older was the night we would open our presents and have family time. Then as they grew and married or developed relationships, the scheduling became more difficult each year, and after the grandsons were born it got worse. She felt at times we played second fiddle to everyone else at Christmas. Our next to last Christmas was a disaster. We had begun to have our time together on Christmas night because we thought everyone would be free, but that night we weren't together for more than thirty minutes. She was so upset because once again it felt like everyone else was more important than her or us.

The last Christmas she decided to play Dirty Santa. I hate this game and said that I would prefer that we get the kids each one nice gift and they could go together and get us each a gift. That way it would be about the same expense and more money could be spent on the grandsons. Nothing good ever comes from that game and it has nothing to do with the spirit of giving or the joy of receiving.

Certainly many people enjoy playing Dirty Santa. It has just been my experience at different parties and family get-togethers that arguments and disagreements occur over rules and who gets what gift. Although I thought I made it perfectly clear this was not what I wanted to do, the family decided otherwise. Nothing major happened while playing the game. However, there were disagreements about the rules and how many times something got passed. The grandsons were tired and the combination of rushing home, playing the game, and the uncertainty of the gifts, made it a difficult night.

Where golf had become a lightning rod for her in our marriage, Christmas had become that for me. It may seem silly that Christmas could or should be something that could cause strife in a marriage because that goes against the spirit and reason of the season. It is sad that we let this happen with us. The part that breaks my heart is that the last family Christmas we had together will be my least favorite.

THE LAST YEARS

This time frame from Craig's graduation in 2004 until four years later would be our greatest roller coaster ride. Things changed quickly and at times almost daily. We would have great moments and then try each other's patience to the breaking point. Financially, we paid cash for many of our home repairs, came into some money, paid off her credit cards, took lots of vacations, and many times seemed to be drawing closer together. Her attitudes toward me at moments seemed to be softer and more loving, but there would be times when you could feel the undercurrent of uneasiness.

Describing it all now brings a flow of emotions that makes it difficult to convey. I was always afraid that after all of the children were gone, she would indeed leave. There was the hope from me that when we were alone we could find the relationship that brought us together in the first place and build on that. Never in our marriage did I ever tell her we couldn't do something she really wanted to do no matter the cost. Making her happy was important to me, as well as just wanting to keep the peace and having a relationship with her. This may have led to many money problems through the years and at the end as we tried to dig ourselves out of a hole.

By 2005, I was working full-time as a traveling notary closer. Of all the occupations I have had in my life, I am the most talented at this. Now most of my career was in some type of sales, and I can do that well, but I am very good at this and get requested from agents and companies to do their closings. Basically what I do is bring refinance mortgage paperwork to you, explain it, have you sign in all the right places, and notarize it. It is a great job because I don't set the appointment, don't sell the loan, and don't have to work up the papers. The down side is that I drive over one hundred thousand miles every year in my car all over the state of Oklahoma. The hours are screwy because someone else sets the time and place for the closing.

Appointments could be set for any time of the day or night. I have closed loans at six thirty in the morning and as late as ten thirty at night. Traveling the entire state of Oklahoma meant that there were nights that I didn't get home until after ten or later. Much like in the beginning of our marriage, she was left alone at night. Many spouses work shifts that don't allow them to be home in the evening or work two jobs to help make in ends met. Couples either make the adjustment to this lifestyle, or it tears them apart. Because I enjoyed my job, was making a solid income, and we were doing things, I felt that she would understand and be there for me.

On the evenings that I was home, I encouraged her to go do things with me, such as dining out, a movie, or walking around the mall. It never mattered what we did when I was home. I only wanted to spend time with her. If we did stay home, for the most part we sat at separate TVs watching different shows. I never was into *Dancing with the Stars*, *The Bachelor*, or *American Idol*. On the other hand, in all the years we were married, she never once sat down and watched a baseball or football game with me unless we were entertaining. We did watch movies together at home, but in the end, even that time was less and less. They say opposites attract, and that may be true, but these must be individuals who want and need their separate interest to maintain a healthy relationship, and that was not us.

It was also hard to schedule anything because I never knew sometimes until the last minute if I was going somewhere or not. Many plans were altered or lost so that I could go to a closing. I told you earlier in the book that when people are good at what they do, the negatives don't really matter, and that was true here. I was good at what I did and couldn't understand that for so many years she had wanted me to find something I enjoyed and stay with what would pay well, and now she wanted me to find something else. Since I didn't have a four-year degree and was fifty-three, it was difficult to find an eight-to-five job Monday through Friday that would support us, but I did try, and nothing seemed to be there. I left jobs before where I had nothing lined up and vowed never to do that again.

The first vacation she and I had been on by ourselves since the first year we were married was to Santa Fe,

New Mexico. This was a four-day trip over her birthday. We had heard from friends and family it was a great place to visit and had tons of things to do. Not every place is the same for everyone, and although it was a good time, it wasn't really up our alley. We visited many of the art galleries and shops and enjoyed the beautiful work and craftsmanship of the local artists, but where some people could do that for days, we were finished at one. We next went up to Taos and browsed the local shops; it was a little more relaxed. We neither one had been to Angel Fire where many of our friends went to ski, so even though there was no snow, we went to look around. There was a rule we had on trips when it came to eating: we couldn't eat at any restaurant we could eat at home. Asking the locals was always a good idea, and we got a tip on a Mexican place that was outstanding. My uncle told me of a nice but expensive place downtown, a steak house he had been to several times.

Her birthday was the day we went to Taos. When we got back in town, we had been gone all day and really needed to go to the hotel to take a shower and change clothes. At this time, I weighed fifty pounds more than I do now, and when I hadn't eaten, I got dizzy and light-headed. Since it was her birthday, she wanted to get dressed up before we went downtown to eat. All I could think about was that I needed to eat right then. When we went into the restaurant, she was visibly upset since it was a nice place and she felt we weren't properly dressed. After viewing the menu and seeing the state she was in, I told her we should go, but we stayed and had a miserable dinner, and it took a major hit on our eating budget. This was a time I should have respected her wishes not only because it was her birthday, but it would have been the right thing to do. I apologized all night for my actions, and although she said it was okay, it wasn't, and I knew it.

The next year we went to San Diego and Las Vegas. It was a great trip until the very end when once again I did something. While in San Diego, all I wanted to do was go to a Padres baseball game. She reluctantly agreed to go. Personally, I thought in May it would be warm and sunny. When we got to the game after flying in that day, it was cold and we were not prepared for it at the game. Without hot chocolate, we couldn't have stayed as long as we did. We ate at several great restaurants, visited the world famous zoo, took a ferry ride around the bay, and visited the old lighthouse. Riding in the car with me has never been one of her favorite things, so driving up the coast to see the ocean sights was interesting.

The ocean has never held any special magic for me as it does for her. If you have seen one large body of water, you have seen them all. I just don't get the thrill! There is a scenic highway that goes from San Diego to LA that my mom and grandparents had talked about, so that was the route we chose. Since the time they went, however, everything between the highway and the ocean was now blocked by homes and businesses. Still we made several stops, drove up near LA, and saw some beautiful scenery. Any time we could stop and look over cliffs and see the ocean, she seemed to light up. Those four days went as smoothly as any time we have ever had, and we both enjoyed our time together.

From there we flew to Las Vegas. We had been there once before when I won a trip while selling cars right before Craig was born. She was about five months pregnant at the time, and we mostly stayed at the hotel. This time we were going to visit all the hotels, see the sights, and go to a couple of shows. We signed up for a presentation for a time share of new apartments and in the process got tickets to two shows. Since we stayed just off the strip, we shuttled each day over to different hotels and took in the sights. I don't think there was a major casino we didn't see. We walked all day twice and ate at great restaurants. The *Rat Pack Review* was one of the shows, and it was outstanding.

We drove over to Hoover Dam and then to Lake Mead for a ferry ride. While we were there, I sincerely don't remember a single minute I didn't enjoy being with her. Gambling is not one of her favorite pastimes, but she seems to be lucky at it when she does. She would play the penny slots, and when she won, she would bring me some of the winnings to play roulette. Once, she set in to play and used her favorite number five and hit several nice spins. When she was having a good time, it was a joy to be around her. We went downtown one evening to watch the light show and listen to the music and never played a dime. The fun was being with each other. Vegas was a great trip in every way for us until it was time to leave Sunday morning.

Because we had played so much roulette, we were given a complimentary breakfast that morning. Our plane left around ten thirty, and we had a rental car to return, so we should have skipped breakfast and gone to the airport. Taking the rental car back took longer than it should have because I missed the exit and went eight miles out of the way. By the time it was turned in and we loaded onto the shuttle and got to the airport, it was too late to catch our plane. The next plane we could get on was four thirty in the afternoon. When I called to let the kids know what had happened, they were almost amazed I was still alive! Then, to make things worse, our connection flight was delayed, causing us to have to wait till midnight for a straight-though flight home. This is the type of thing she normally became upset with me about, but instead she took it all in stride and never complained or said a cross word. In fact, she really saved the day for us. When she learned what had happened, she got to the attendants right away to figure out how we were getting home. For both of us, I think this was not only a great vacation but the kind we had always wanted to experience.

Our last long vacation was to Montana. I have a cousin who lives there, and they had wanted us to come up for years. They absolutely love living there and enjoy showing off the part they live in. We planned for a year to go, and she had everything planned up to Montana; then we would play it by ear coming home.

Now the only time I would ever go there was in July because I hate cold and snow! On the Fourth of July, for several years my family has hosted my mother's side of the family for lunch. Any of the relatives who lived close by got a chance to see each other, and every so often one of our long-distance cousins would show up. That year it was on a Friday, so as soon as it was over, we would be off to Montana. All of the family knew we were leaving and made early exits so we could hit the road.

That night as we drove through Kansas we were treated to fireworks shows as we passed by the towns and cities. It was if we had our own private screening in the car, and it was an exceptional and romantic moment. We spent the night in Kansas then headed for the black hills of South Dakota. I can't even begin to tell you how much she enjoyed this part of the trip. Her camera was on overdrive as we took pictures of everything we saw for what we thought was the vacation of our lives. This is beautiful country with rich history and great sites to visit. On our way to Mount Rushmore, we drove through the national park and saw up close buffalo by the hundreds. The road winds through the park, and every so often you go through an opening and can see the faces on the mount. It is an inspirational place to visit. After that, we went on a cave tour, saw an indoor waterfall, and visited the Crazy Horse monument. This area is one of the two places we wished we could have spent more time.

Montana is not only a long way away, but it is also one big state once you get there. When we arrived that evening, they had dinner all ready for us on the back patio. It was almost too perfect—excellent food, great company, incredible weather, and a breathtaking view. My cousin and her husband are not only great hosts, but they are also the nicest people you will ever meet, and we have always treasured their company. They took us on a river raft ride that, according to my former wife, was her favorite part of the trip and then up to Glacier National Park and hiking up in the mountains. These were three great days, and it only made us wish we could have stayed longer. When we got ready to leave, they told us of a small town that had a neat candy store in the middle of nowhere but not that far out of the way. If there was any type of candy to be had, this place had it! We spent more than we should have here, but it was worth the visit. On the way down to Colorado, we went to see Yellowstone and Grand Teton Mountain. Yellowstone, with its geysers and boiling springs, is a must-see, but the mountain didn't do much for me.

Unfortunately, when we hit Denver, it was during rush-hour traffic. I thought she would have a nervous breakdown before we could get to a hotel. I drive every day all day long and have had fewer accidents than her, but she absolutely hates to ride with me and can drive not only me but any of the children crazy if she has to ride with them. She will tell you which way to go, where to park, and if there is a car fifty yards away headed in your direction. All of the children cringe when they have to drive with their mother anywhere. When we got to the hotel and settled in, I sat her down and told her she just couldn't keep making me a basket case when we rode together, and she said she just never trusted my driving. I tried to explain that when she was with me, I always tried to be extra careful. This did nothing to relieve her fears or change her mind. After she calmed down, we went over to Mineral Springs City to see the shops and have all-you-could-eat catfish.

The next day we were headed home, and it would be an all-day trip. We stopped to see several sites and again got into a great Mexican restaurant. We had to get home by Saturday night because I was playing golf on my last day of vacation, which was Sunday. Saying this was a sore spot with her doesn't begin to explain how unhappy she was that we had to be home early so I could play golf. On our other vacations, I never asked to get back early so I could play, and on the one after this, I never requested it. She felt that for some reason this was her vacation more than it was ours, and the fact that I wanted to get back to play was totally unacceptable. Neither my children nor most individuals I have asked ever thought it was an unreasonable request. It would, however, be held to my head as if it were a gun for the remainder or our marriage.

This was a great vacation and one we will both always remember fondly. Her favorite part, as I said, was the river raft, but mine was the times we stopped and had lunches together with the leftover food from the Fourth. We would stop at a roadside park or some small town park, fix sandwiches, and be with each other. Once, we took a long walk around the park, held hands, and took in the moment together. I always would look at her and tell her I loved her and wanted her to be with me.

Our last trip was to Shreveport over Labor Day 2008. We left on Friday when she got off work and drove about halfway there and spent the night. Up the next morning, we headed for Louisiana. Someone we both graduated with lived there, so if we could just remember their last name, we were going to look them up and see the sights. Shreveport has an outdoor mall by the river with great shops and restaurants. We spent most of the afternoon there going from shop to shop. When we did get ready to go, the car had a flat. We had to find a tire shop. It was late Saturday afternoon, so finding not only some place open but that could fix it then was a challenge. Sticking to our rule about dining out, we were told of a great local place to visit, and once again the information was on the money. After going to the show, we went back to the hotel room, and I began to look for the couple we knew by looking at all the names in the phone book. Finally I found them at ten thirty and called. They were having a party, so we went to their place till two in the morning. Tom and Melody are two of our favorite people when we get to see them.

Sunday we slept in then saw the historical sites downtown before going to the casino. We didn't play much and didn't win at all. Melody invited us over for a swim and drinks. That evening we went back to the mall to see it at night with all the lights on the river, and it was a memorable moment. From a romantic stance, it was a wonderful. Few times in our marriage had we been together like we were those two nights. Monday we headed home, stopping off in Dallas to see my one of my best friends, Randy, and his wife, Joann, for lunch. There are several antique shops along I-35, and we hit them all. If you had told me that only four months later she would inform me our marriage was over at that point, I would never have believed it could be true. I'm not sure how two people could have had a better weekend than we had, but perhaps it was only that from my perspective.

I went down the vacation slideshow so that you would know that as a couple we were doing things together. Travel and vacations were something she always wanted to do, and we were doing them. She even went to Puerto Rico with Renee and Jeremy. The question was how all of this traveling was being paid for. We got tax-return money each year because of all the deductions from my job. This money was for whatever trip we wanted to take. The problem was that either it wasn't enough or we spent part of it on car repairs or other emergencies. Out would come the credit cards, and away we would go, thinking that we would only use what we needed to and would pay it off as soon as we could. Sometimes we would come into money or have good months and pay some off or pay them down, but there was usually something breaking down each month, or we needed the money for other things.

We were eating out more often, going to shows, and buying things we both could have waited for and done without. If we wanted to do something, many times we did it whether we could afford to or not. Our financial situation was such that the only way to get out was to bring more money into the home. Not wanting her to work a second job and knowing whatever she did part-time wouldn't make that big of a difference, I looked for a second career. Being in the mortgage industry, I saw many people doing what is called a reverse mortgage. At the time, companies would use brokers to help find clients. Brokers were then paid a fee for that service. I set up a business and had companies lined up to send people to. It took about a year to get it all in place; then in August of 2008 when I was to see my first client, Congress passed a bill and killed my new business in one day. The time and investment were gone.

In the meantime, our closings had begun to slow down with less and less people refinancing their homes. We were still paying all our bills; we just weren't making any progress on paying them off or down. Since people were making money on the Internet, I sent off for a course on how to set up a website and sell products and services. It seemed there were lots of ways to supplement your income with the Internet, and it could the perfect solution. I would work it in my spare time and do it at home. The problem was that I was not very computer savvy, and many things that seemed simple became overwhelming. For two months, I worked every spare minute trying to set up a site and place products that people could purchase. The further I got into it, the more it began to frustrate me. Since she works on computers all day long, I thought she would come and help, but as always, when it came to doing something together, it was a struggle.

She is a very analytical person and has to read everything about what she is doing before she acts on anything. So when she came to help, *if* she came to help, it would take her an agonizing amount of time to either assist me or say she didn't know what to do. From the time I started until the first of December when I gave up, I nearly had two nervous breakdowns from the stress of trying to do it and the pressure of wanting to pay off our bills to make her happy. Each time she would come and comfort me until I got better, but I could feel her uneasiness.

I had kept in close touch with my old insurance company and went in to see if there was a way I could work there around my closing schedule. These were the most wonderful people you could ever meet, and when I explained my situation, they said they could work something out. She was less than thrilled about my return to the insurance industry since twice I had not done that well at it. I tried to explain this time would be different because I had the closing income to rely on and there would be less pressure. I had plenty of time, and if I was halfway successful, it could pull us out of the hole in time. If she had said, "Let's do this," and, "How can I help?" it would have made a huge difference for me, but because of my past, she was skeptical, and with just cause. I knew for some reason this time would be different, and it has been. I've done well even with the events that happened in my life. Had she stayed and believed in me more, we would have been even better positioned to take care of our obligations than we are now.

Being together simply for monetary purposes is, of course, no way for anyone to be married, and I would not have wanted her to stay for just that reason. I would have liked one last chance to prove to her with all the changes I was making personally and professionally she could love me as much as I loved her.

THE LAST SEPARATION:
Part One

December of 2008 was perhaps the worst month in all the years we were married. Three events happened during the month that, looking back on now, I used poor judgment. Alone, each one might have been overlooked or forgiven, but put together, it was too much for her to handle. There were reasons at the time that I did what I did; however, that doesn't change the fact that I made the wrong choices.

Her company Christmas party was always an important event. Many years she either helped plan or coordinate the function. Whenever she was involved, I always thought it was a better party. She has a flair for planning. We went every year, and one year I even helped decorate. The people she works with are outstanding and enjoyable to be around. She delighted in a good party, and it was her chance to dance. Dancing was never one of my strong suits, and she never really liked the way I danced and told me so on more than one occasion. When I should have danced with her, I didn't, simply to avoid the criticism. This is not the mistake I made that year. I didn't go at all. I had a closing that night, and because we needed the money, I went. In retrospect, it was more important to be with her that night. The funny thing was that years ago I would never thought about going to the closing, but somewhere along the line I changed. It was a great disappointment to her that I wasn't there and chose my job over her again.

Either at the party or at her work, she won a free night at a hotel downtown. We planned a Saturday evening of going to dinner, listening to music, and being together. This was something we needed badly. The dinner was at Toby Keith's restaurant, a favorite place of ours to eat. Eating out together had become a quiet time for us as we struggled to have a conversation with each other. After dinner, we strolled over to some sights and listened to a small band playing at Mickey Mantle's, a local restaurant. The silence was even more deafening. The communication between us had disappeared. It was bitter cold that night, and as we walked from place to place, we never held hands or cuddled to keep warm. We went back to the hotel and got ready for bed. She had brought my favorite nightgown and had it on when I came out of the bathroom. I hadn't seen that black negligee all year and had to go to a hotel for her to break it out. Normally I would have been delighted, but not this time. I was upset that once again we had to be somewhere else for her to act like she wanted to be with me. This was the next to last time we would make love, and both times we simply went through the motions.

I no longer was doing the Internet business, had gone back to the insurance job, and was mentally drained. A weekend with her should have been all that was on my mind. It wasn't. Sunday was golf day. I thought I needed to get away for a few hours to help with my sanity. She, of course, asked me not to go this one Sunday, but I went anyway. All she wanted was to spend the day with me and feel important, and I couldn't give that to her that day. In the moment, it is hard to realize that one is being selfish, but upon reflection, it is obvious. That weekend might have once again saved our marriage, but my mental state of mind prevented me from again doing the right thing for her.

For more years than I can remember, we had gone to dinner with close friends, Terry and Monica and then to the show for New Year's Eve. Some years other couples would come along. The year before, we went to dinner, to the casino, to a movie, and out for ice cream. The four of us could not have had a better time. Terry has been one of my closest friends for over thirty-eight years, and he has known her almost that long. Our last New Year's, once again I was scheduled to do a closing that late afternoon. I was not happy about having to go but felt we needed the money, so I went. The closing was delayed, and I was going to get back later than I had expected, so I called to let her know where I was and when I would be there. The tone in her voice I can still feel as she coldly told me they weren't going to wait for me at the restaurant and were going ahead without me. After I got there, everything seemed to be normal, but she was distant as usual. We went to the show with my sister and her husband since our friend Terry wasn't feeling well and went home early.

When the show was over, they had somewhere else to be, so we headed home. On the way, I suggested that we go downtown for the ball dropping at midnight and see the party atmosphere. We had never gone downtown for New Year's Eve, so this would be a new and fun experience for us both. Once again it was bitter cold as we walked around. I wasn't sure what was chillier, the air or our feelings about one another. While we were there, it seemed to be an enjoyable time between us as we strolled downtown and listened to the music until midnight. The ball dropped, and as most couples do, we kissed. The kiss was more of a token kiss than one with any feeling or passion. I remember thinking at that moment, *When was the last time we actually had a loving and romantic kiss?* All I could come up with was four months earlier in Shreveport.

From New Year's Day until she uttered the words that began the book twenty-five days later, it was a difficult time for both of us. I was working hard to get ready to start selling insurance, closing loans, and trying to figure out how we could get out of debt as soon as possible. I felt alone and isolated at times from her, and that made each day more difficult. I was focused on doing well and solving our financial problems, but for the first time in the marriage, she could have cared less and spent money on things she wanted. Her reasoning was that I spent all this money on golf so it was time for her to enjoy whatever she wanted, no matter the cost. I have argued that I spent just as much on her as I did on golf, but she would never in a million years admit that was true. Not once in our marriage did I fail to get her a Christmas present even if she didn't get me one. I never missed a Valentine's Day (the year before I spent two days looking for a chocolate pearl ring because she wanted one), and we always did something special for our anniversary. I took her to dinner and to the show every chance I got—or anywhere else she asked to go. I would have done anything she wanted to do if she had just asked.

Some may say if I really knew her I would have known what she wanted. I can't tell you how many times I asked her if there was anything she wanted to do other than what we were doing, and she never mentioned doing any of the things she does now. That was just not who we had been for thirty-three years, so how was I supposed to know if she didn't tell me! All the things she does now are things I would have enjoyed doing with her if she had only said something. People may change through the course of a marriage; however, that is not an excuse to dissolve the marriage only an opportunity for them to experience new horizons with each other if they are willing to try.

After New Year's Day, which was the last time we were together, we seldom hugged or kissed or showed any emotion toward each other except frustration. We never got mad to the point it was a fight. One of us would simply walk away to avoid the conflict. A friend once told me they were amazed at how little we seemed to not get along, as if it was something out of the ordinary. Learning what each one needed to do to keep the status quo intact was something we had learned through the years I suppose. Looking back now, perhaps a few good shouting matches would have done us some good, but I doubt it. That was not her style or the way she liked to handle things.

After almost a month of token kisses goodnight, always being fully dressed around me, and showing me no physical connection, on a Sunday night I finally confronted her. I asked her if we were going to have any intimate time together anymore. That was exactly how I worded it, knowing that if I said it any other way she would be upset. I pointed out that we weren't talking, that my picture she took down in her room to do something with never got put back up, and that she never called me during the day to see how I was doing. She remembers me asking if we were going to have sex anymore. This was the moment she must have been waiting for, hearing only what she wanted to hear. At that moment she seemed to find all the courage and conviction that had been lacking. It was her opportunity to say, "No. I don't love you, I am not sure I ever really ever loved you, and I need out of this marriage."

As I heard the words, all my worst fears were about to come to pass. I stood leaning up against the dresser holding on as if somehow it would keep me from falling through a dark hole. The words I spoke at this point would only be a guess; yet I'm sure I must have pleaded my case for a short time before I made my way to the dining room table and began what would be nine months of crying. All the emotion I had built up inside me came out as I uncontrollably wept for hours. She came to calm me down. I tried to talk to her, but I simply couldn't stop crying and pleading for her not to go and to give me one more chance. Saying she was glad it was out in the open and relieved, this was the only course of action for her now. It wasn't that she didn't care for me or even love me in some way; it was that she wasn't *in* love with me. How one little word can change the entire meaning of a phase. There are many kinds of love, but saying, "I love you," to your spouse should mean, "You are the person I'm in love with."

The next morning I had to leave early to be in eastern Oklahoma for a closing. I asked that she call me as soon as she could because I was so upset. It didn't come, so I called her in a complete emotional breakdown. What would I do without her? I pleaded on the phone. Who was going to want me? I'm fifty-two, overweight, and losing my hair. Who was going to want to be with me? Who would go with me on New Year's Eve? What about the holidays or our anniversary? More and more questions kept coming to mind. Since she was at work, she couldn't talk long but tried to reassure me that it would all work out and that this was best for both of us.

Since that day, everybody, including her, has told me what I should do. Everyone had an opinion of what I should do at this point, but no one asked me what I wanted. I didn't want to lose my wife, my friend, lover, and the person I hoped would be my life-long companion. People said everything from putting all her stuff on the front porch and having her come and get it, changing all the locks and letting her fend for herself, to telling her go jump in a lake and drown. I have from the start tried to deal with this on my own terms. A close friend told me to listen to myself first and do what I thought was best for me. Many times I went against standard advice and did what I thought was right for me. It wasn't going to matter what I did really. I was miserable. All I could do was look in the mirror and know I was the kind of person I wanted to be through this most days and that I was doing the best I could to save my marriage.

I tried to get her to agree not to tell anyone for a while; although she agreed to wait for a short time, I was informed again there was no turning back for her. Over the next few weeks between pleading my case and doing everything I could think to make her change her mind, we would become emotionally upset with one another. Many things on both sides were said that should never have been shared, and we were both hurt, and it damaged our relationship further. I was so upset on several occasions that I could barely express myself, and my emotions would bring me to a point of fist pounding and loud exchanges. This would only make it worse because she hated it when my voice got loud and animated.

We were still appearing in public together at many functions. It was difficult since I could no longer even touch the small of her back or hold her hand. There may not be anything more agonizing than being next to someone that you want to hold and kiss and not be able to touch them at all. On several occasions, I literally walked around almost all night when she was close with my hands in my pockets. There are no words to express the hurt and loneliness you can feel when someone you love doesn't want you at all.

We agreed not to tell the kids for a while and to do it together. Then one Saturday morning when I was gone out of town, out of the blue she told Craig all by herself. When I got home and she told me, I about went nuts. How could she do that without me and the girls there? It was at that point and from then on that she would act with whatever actions she thought were best for her. Since she had told Craig and was leaving to go somewhere, I drove to Renee's and told her what was going on. She had seen me upset at her house a couple of times in the past few weeks when I had been there, but her mother told her I was just tired. When I told her, she became understandably upset. Again, Renee is a very faith-based person and has always felt this was wrong and didn't understand why this was happening. Plus, she was upset that her mother had told Craig and not all of them together.

On the way home, I called Christy and Craig and told them to meet me at the house. We sat down in the den, and I calmly explained that their mother was leaving and wanted a divorce because she didn't love me and said she never really loved me and needed out of the marriage. Craig took it better at first, partly because he already knew, and I think to a degree he thought it would be better for me. Christy, on the other hand, was not at all happy that her mother had told Craig first and without her and Renee being present. This was not the way it was supposed to have been handled, but I didn't think it was fair for Craig to be the only one to know, and since their mother had started the process, I would finish it. When she got home, I explained I had told the girls, and she asked me why I didn't wait until she could be there!

The next few weeks I don't even remember except I know I was upset all the time and struggled to work at my jobs. The days became more and more difficult as she shut me out of her life completely. The hardest part for me was that I was married one day and cut out the next. As most marriages end, there is a time when things are going bad. There may be fighting or ugliness to each other, so when the end comes, everyone is ready to go their separate ways. I got the news, and the next day I didn't have a wife. I couldn't know who she talked to, where she was going, or who she was with. How do you go from knowing everything about your spouse to not knowing anything in one day? I have never gotten over that and will never understand. For thirty-three years we were together, and then we weren't. I couldn't handle it.

One night she went out with two of her friends from work. It was again a time that I couldn't know where she was going or when she would be back. What I did that night I don't really remember, but I got home around eleven, and she wasn't home. Although I wasn't supposed to, I called her cell phone and got no answer. I was having such a hard time not knowing where she was that I would drive myself crazy thinking about what and who she might be with. Midnight came and went, and she was still not home. I looked out the window every other minute or when any car drove by to see if it was her.

When she finally got home at two, there was another car behind hers, and they slowly drove past the house. I went outside to see what in the world was going on. As I approached the cars, I could see her girlfriend was driving one car but that a man was driving her car with her in it. I ripped open the car door, and I'm sure the man thought I was about to come unglued on him. My temper has already been talked about, so she didn't know what to expect. I told the man to get out of her car. I then got in the car with her and drove off. I was ranting and raving at her in the car about being out with another man as she tried to explain. I was in no mood for any explanation and didn't care why he was in the car. After we drove down the street and back, the people were still there waiting on her to make sure she was okay. She got out and assured them that no matter how mad I got, she was in no danger and that I would calm down in a bit and she would explain it all to me.

After they left, she gave me the story of what happened that night. I'm still not sure I believe all that she told me about that night, but I felt bad about the way I acted toward total strangers. It was the first time I had let my jealousy get the best of me, and I vowed I wouldn't let that happen again. The next day I bought her and both of them a nice bottle of wine and took it to them with a note of apology. Emotions can make you do things that normally you would never think you would do, but that does not excuse my behavior that night.

I might as well tell you about one other event that happened during this time. The exact time it happened I'm not sure, and it really isn't important, only the event. One Saturday we had a terrible argument about what she was doing and with whom. I was so upset after we talked I must have called everyone I could think of to tell them how mad I was with her. When I got home, I was furious at her because I felt that she had unnecessarily hurt me and I needed to lash back at her. We had two sets of wedding pictures in the hall cabinet. I took the extra set to the bedroom and began to tear them into pieces to show her that it was over between us. Then I found our vacation pictures, and any that had us together, I cut a line between us. When she got home, they were all laid out on the bed for her to see.

I hurt her many times during the separation, but I know this was one of the deepest hurts. She lashed back at me by tearing up all the letters I had written to her during this time. I was devastated. She couldn't believe I would simply tear up the wedding pictures. My emotions were so uncontrollable at this point that I couldn't make myself stop no matter what I did. I knew it was wrong to tear up the pictures. I just couldn't stop. That night I not only cried because she was leaving but because I had hurt her again, and I had never wanted to do that to her.

The kids were each dealing with their mother but not very well. They were upset that their mother was taking so much away from them, that she had hurt me, and that she had not been truthful with us through the years. I tried to explain that she loved them very much and this had nothing to do with them, but it was difficult for them to accept. Since their mother was telling them almost nothing, it made it even worse. We disagreed about what the children should know from the very beginning. They were grown adults, and I felt they should be told as much as we could share because this was affecting their lives and it would help them understand. There was very little I didn't share and almost nothing she did. I was around them more, and because I was upset most of the time, she felt this worked against her, but I always tried to make sure that even when she upset me and I told them what she had done that they needed to remember that she was their mother and to treat her accordingly.

There seemed to be no way things could be worse. Then I got a call, and our whole world was shaken to the very core. Events can change and alter lives in many ways, and this would test every part of our faith and understanding for each other and as a family. The separation was hard enough; this simply brought more emotion to an already unbearable time. I had lost my wife and would nearly lose my daughter.

THE ACCIDENT

On March 9, 2009, Renee was involved in a horrible and tragic car accident. Short of your child dying, there is nothing more terrifying to a parent than to see your daughter hooked up to all kinds of devices to keep her alive. The feeling of helplessness is indescribable unless you have been there. Being told your daughter has a fifty-percent chance of not making it can rock you to your foundation. How does one comprehend that type of information? It came to us so unexpectedly that I never had time to process it at first because I was focused on what the doctor was saying, and along with Jeremy (her husband) asking what was being done and what could be done, it didn't hit me until later that night.

In writing this book, I knew this chapter would have to come up eventually. Since the purpose is to explain what happened in the marriage, I won't go into the injuries and treatments Renee received. I will take you through a series of events that happened that made dealing with this time difficult for me, the children, and their mother. It is an absolute miracle that Renee is alive, and if you didn't know she was in a car wreck, it would never show. Renee, like her mother, is a very determined and focused individual who, as I said before, has great faith in God. One never knows when God calls someone home, but I never once felt it was her time or that she wouldn't pull through.

Renee was in the hospital for nearly two months. They said she would be there for up to four. Time has a way of playing tricks on the mind when everything in your life is turned upside down. While she was there, many events happened between my former wife, me, and the other two children. Having a child in the trauma wing of the hospital is trying enough. Add to that the stress of the separation; it was mentally and emotionally exhausting. The time Renee spent in the hospital seemed an eternity at times, and this time seemed even longer in terms of the separation.

Many times over these two months there would be great differences between us. What could have brought us all closer together as a family only caused more strife and magnified the difference between her and us. I will tell the story and actions that happened as they unfolded those two months. There is no way to tell this part of the tale and make their mother look good in the light. She knew as I did from the beginning that Renee would pull through, and maybe that affected her judgment. Only she can answer that question. Nothing was going to stop her from ending our marriage and doing the things she felt it was okay for her to do, not even her daughter being in the hospital. This was a difficult time for me, and there are things I did toward her I am not proud of to this day, but many of my actions were reactions to the actions and decisions she made.

The first night Renee was in the hospital, there were so many friends and family that came to be with her and to see about us. Anyone who knew us at all knew how we felt about all of our children and would have known how difficult this would be for us. The outpouring of love and concern is still amazing to me. My daughter had touched so many lives, and they came to be with her that day and many more to come. Some of our close friends, Dana and Laura, came that night late in the evening. We told them about the accident, how Renee was doing, the treatment she was receiving, and then just began to chitchat. The wreck happened on a Monday morning. Dana, Laura, and my former wife were scheduled to leave on Friday to go on a cruise with the Jimmy Buffet fan club. Our conversation somehow got tuned to all the things they would be doing on the trip. As I sat and listened to my former wife talk about all the things she had bought for the trip, how she would decorate her cabin door and the toga outfit she was going to wear, I couldn't believe what I was hearing. I got up and walked away as if when I came back that perhaps I was just imagining this, but the conversation was still about all the things she was going to do on the trip. So I left again because I wasn't sure I could control my emotions at that point.

When they left, we went to see our grandson at the adjacent hospital. By grace, he was spared any injuries and was at the children's hospital for observation. There is a long tunnel between the two hospitals, and when we reached that point, I informed her that there was no way she could go on the trip! This is not what she wanted to hear. Her first words were, "Well, if she is all right by Thursday, then I should be able to go." I reminded her that our daughter earlier in the day had been given a fifty-percent chance to live and that she was hooked up to all those devices to keep her alive. This trip was something she was really looking forward to, and she just didn't want to accept the fact that she couldn't go. It may be at this moment her mind simply couldn't function in a rational way, and I know deep down she knew she couldn't go. She just didn't want to accept it or be told by me she couldn't. The discussion in the breezeway was loud and emotionally packed as we argued. Finally she accepted the fact she had to stay; she didn't like it but knew there was no other decision.

The second day was a day filled with great relief as it became clear that Renee was going to live. The place was crowded with people and more food than any one family could eat. It would be entertaining in a way to tell all the stories about those first few days. I was still trying to keep abreast of all that was going on with her care, seeing her when we could go in, and visiting with all the friends and family. There were times during the day when we both would be together at her bedside or listening to the doctor, and I would put my arm around her or hold her hand because we were Renee's parents and I felt we needed to be there for her and each other. This was, however, not what she wanted, and that evening I was told that while we were both there for Renee, we were not there as a couple or man and wife, but only as her separate parents. I nearly lost my daughter, and one day later her mother is driving home the point one more time that we are not together no matter what the circumstance. If she had a call or if someone wanted to talk to her, she would walk away so that I couldn't know who she was talking to or about what. The hurt and loneliness of that can never be expressed, to be shut out from a life you shared everything with at a time like this seemed almost cruel.

On Thursday, we had reached a point of exhaustion. We had been up for the most part of three days with very little sleep. I went that day to close a loan and do a little insurance work; she had gone to her office to do what needed to be done. Each evening the hospital would have a shift change between six and eight, and we couldn't go in to see Renee during that time. Again the waiting room was full of family and friends. She had made plans before this happened to go out to dinner with some of her coworkers. Since she didn't tell me anything anymore, I didn't find out about this until the day before. I told her that day and Thursday afternoon that she needed to stay there with us and the family that was there, including her dad, but she would have none of it. She needed to get away. She had made plans and needed to be apart from me for a short time. While I understand the stress she was under, I never understood why it was okay for her to go out with her friends while her daughter was in the trauma unit. She told us that she would be back by eight so she could go and see Renee.

The moment she left, I broke down and had to go to another part of the hospital. Christy and Craig finally found me crying uncontrollably. I just couldn't believe that she would go and leave her family to be with other people at a time like this.

When eight thirty rolled around, she didn't come back, and by eight forty-five my children made me go home because I was so upset. We all tried to call her on her cell phone, but she never answered. Her daughter was in the trauma wing of the hospital, and she didn't have her cell out where she can hear or see that it was ringing? From eight fifteen until she showed back up at nine thirty, no one could reach her. When she did arrive, Craig laid into her out in the lobby just as she walked in. I would never encourage my children to be disrespectful to their mother, and I'm sure he went over the line, but this time I didn't feel sorry for her at all. Her excuse was the restaurant was loud and that she couldn't hear the phone and lost track of time. I have tried many times to justify her actions that night, but I have never been able to. Christy and Craig were unhappy about their mother's actions. When Renee found out, she was upset with her mother's selfishness. Whether it was right or wrong for her not to be at the hospital is dependent on one's own perspective.

During this time, it was difficult for me as I couldn't understand all that was going on around me. I wanted my wife, my daughter to recover, to be successful in both my jobs, and to find a way out of our financial mess. This at times was more than I could hold up to emotionally, I would simply go home, sit in the car, or find a quiet place to cry for hours. People reminded me time after time that things would be fine and that time would heal all wounds. You may hear the words and believe they are true, but at that moment it didn't seem possible. Had my faith been in a better place with God, I could have handled it better in the beginning. Only really after the divorce did I finally begin to let God take control and find some peace.

For her, this period was even more difficult as she tried to deal with me and be there for Renee. As I said before, she is a person who needs to be in control, and at the hospital many times that was not the case. Renee was married, and her husband was the one who was taking care of Renee. Jeremy is the type of son-in-law that every parent wants for his or her daughter. As a parent, it is always difficult to let go of your children and, when they are in pain, not to want to be their main caregiver. Jeremy is a respiratory therapist and worked at both hospitals Renee was at and was the most qualified person to handle his wife's recovery. We both were involved with the decisions, but Jeremy had the final word.

I know that I didn't make things any easier for my former wife because of my desire to save the marriage. Her mind was past the point of there being any reconciliation, but I just couldn't keep from trying all of the time to persuade her to stay. We weren't getting any sleep and going around in circles, so she decided to move out in April. I moved in with my sister for several weeks before so that we could have some space and sleep. One problem with her during this time was her not having her cell phone on all the time. Many times all of us tried and tried to reach her, but she wouldn't call back until hours later. One night at my sister's house my nose began to bleed uncontrollably. No matter what I did, I couldn't stop the bleeding. I called her for almost an hour, but she never picked up the phone. By the time I reached my son and he got to me, the stool and bath room had blood everywhere. They took me to the emergency room. I was treated and sent home. I went to my home and waited for her to return. Craig was so upset with his mother that when she did get home late that evening, I made him leave.

Like his dad, his temper at times can get the best of him, and this was not the time or place for him to explode on his mother, and I was in no condition to intervene. I was still upset but had calmed down. After I told her what had happened and that I tried desperately to reach her, she simply asked in a puzzled tone why I didn't just lean my head back till it stopped and reminded me she was no longer responsible for me anymore.

When Renee came out of the trauma unit and was sent to rehab, her mother had become self-absorbed. Almost nothing was more important as whatever she wanted to do. One day I had to go to McAlester to do a closing, and Renee was not doing well, so I called every hour to talk to Jeremy to check on her condition. I called my wife to see if she could get off a little early to go be there, but she was planning a company party that afternoon and said she needed to be there to set things up but would get there when she could. I almost lost my mind. Anyone at her job would have pitched in and helped her out if she would have just asked. That party was not as important as her daughter. After several calls, she finally left and went to the hospital. When I got there, she was mad at me because when she arrived, Jeremy and his mother and sisters were there taking care of Renee, and she wondered why it was all that important for her to be there. She was in charge where she was but not here.

The day she moved out, April 10, Renee was still in the hospital. Through this experience, she wanted Renee to know as little as possible about what was going on with us. In the beginning, that was a good idea. As Renee began to get her wits back, she knew most of what was going on, and Jeremy told her at times what she wanted to know if she asked. Her mother had no idea how much Renee really knew, and when she found out, she was unhappy with all of us that we had told her. It was never our intention to upset Renee during the recovery, but if she wanted to know something, it was better to tell her than not. Although we were having a difficult time living together, I always felt she should have stayed until Renee got out of the hospital. She said it didn't matter, when she left it would be hard for me, and that she needed some peace.

On the day she moved out, she rented a U-Haul and went to the house. I had told her she could take whatever she wanted, so I'm not going to complain about what she took, only her reasoning for taking certain items. It goes back to the mine and our philosophy. She shopped for and bought the vacuum cleaner. Although I had a house and she had a small apartment, she was entitled to it. Same with the iron and board and anything else she felt was hers whether she needed it or not. She kept the best of the furniture and all of the accessories that went with them simply because she felt they were hers more than ours. This is not to say she took everything because she didn't, and most of the things she divided evenly. Instead of having the attitude that she would like to have certain things, she had the feeling she was entitled to them or that they were hers. The only thing I asked to be left intact was the kitchen because I was still paying for it, and she still took a painting over the sink because she either got it from someone at work or bought it there.

Renee had to have a procedure done unexpectedly that day, and no one could reach her mother. Jeremy had called me to let me know what was going on and to tell me that once again they couldn't reach Renee's mother. When I got to the house, they were loading up everything, and I asked her family to wait outside while we talked. I had had it with her never having her phone on and laid into her. She got upset because I was getting on to her and in front of her family, but had her phone been on all this would have been avoided. I told her they were doing a procedure on Renee and we needed to go to the hospital. She replied that she only had the truck for a certain time and needed to finish moving first. I picked up what

I thought were my keys and left. Unfortunately, I picked up her keys as well, and she had to come to the hospital. She didn't even go up to see Renee. It was all about what she needed to do that day.

Jeremy told me that Renee wanted us to watch the movie *Fireproof.* He bought us a copy and asked that we watch it together. One evening when things were quiet at the hospital, we sat down to watch the movie. I asked her to come and sit by me while it played.

"Why do we need to sit by each other?" she asked.

"Because Renee wanted us to," I replied.

Begrudgingly she came to the couch, and I plugged in the movie. Several times during the movie I cried. She never once showed any emotion. When it was over, I asked her what she thought, and she said it was a good movie. About 80 percent of that movie you could have put us up on that screen, and she just thought it was a good movie. I pressed the point that much of that story pertained to us, but there was absolutely no way her mind would ever admit that even if it were true. That was not us, and our situation was different. This movie or any other event was not going to change her mind.

From that point until Renee left the hospital, there were other events that happened. However, the most unforgivable to me happened on the last day Renee was in the hospital. By now she was ready to go home and was impatient to get there. This was causing her to have some anxiety issues. She had asked a close friend to stay with her that last night because she didn't like to be left alone. Jeremy was taking care of Carson, my grandson, and would have to be at the hospital early to get Renee. I called to make sure someone was going to be with her and told her I had to go to Tulsa to close a loan but that I would be home by eight thirty and would stop in and see her. As I got ready to leave Tulsa, I called to make sure all was well. The person who was to stay with her couldn't come, so she called her mom. I told her I would be back by eight thirty and would stop in. When I got into town, I called again only to find her mother wasn't there yet and that another friend was staying with her till her mother got there.

That night she had already made plans to go out with a coworker before Renee called. Most mothers at that point would have cancelled whatever plans if their daughter asked them to come to the hospital. She not only didn't cancel but was going to show up almost one and a half hours later than what she told Renee. I called her and told her just to stay home, and I would go instead. You could tell by the tone of her voice that again she couldn't figure why we were upset or that she thought she had done anything wrong. How she could justify this in her own mind I will never understand, but being somewhere seemed to take priority over her own daughter. While Renee was in the hospital and afterward, this would be true for all of us in the family.

THE SEPARATION:
Part 2

The second part of the separation began with the move out. I was not easy to be with at this point. Emotionally I couldn't accept what was happening to me and felt I hadn't done anything that warranted this to end. Many nights I lay on the floor or in bed holding her picture and begging her and God for her to stay. I pleaded my case over and over hoping to find the right words or phrase that would turn her around. The more we talked, the worse it seemed to be. I couldn't accept the fact that she was leaving and then that she was gone.

The Friday she moved out was Easter weekend. Christy, Craig, and the boys were going to have Easter at the house. This was the only time I didn't invite her to a family gathering. I couldn't see her moving out on Friday and getting to come back over on Sunday to celebrate Easter. She didn't know we were getting together until Renee told her that day at the hospital. She didn't understand why we couldn't be together just as it was before and was upset that we didn't invite her. It didn't seem right that she could leave our home on

Friday and return on Sunday for a family gathering. It was a lonely and sad day for me as this was the first holiday as a family we were not all together. As I sat in my kitchen that day alone after everyone had left, I wasn't sure how I would survive. How would I handle future holidays without her with us?

On Monday morning before she went to work, I took some things over to her. She asked if I wanted to see the apartment. I went in and collapsed on the floor. Here was my wife and the furniture that had been in our house in some apartment. It was more than I could stand as I began to beg her to come home. I cried over and over to please come home. She held me and again told me that wasn't going to happen and that I had to try and control my emotions. She knew this was difficult for me but that there was no other choice for her now.

The next weekend we had planned to go to the Jimmy Buffet concert in Frisco, Texas. We had bought tickets before Renee's accident to attend the party being put on by the COPA chapter. This was one big party, and we both wanted to go. There was much discussion the week leading up to the weekend as to who was going to use the tickets. I wanted to go together and spend some time with each other as a starting point for a new relationship. She wanted to go, but if it was with me, only as friends, and that was begrudgingly. Finally we decided to go together, get a room with double beds, and I volunteered to pay for everything.

It was a strange weekend as we spent the time together, but we were never really spending time together. There were times we spent walking around looking at everyone's party; then she would be gone for long periods of time. Each of the two nights we were there, it was if as we were total strangers when we got to the hotel room. She was so uncomfortable, and I was miserable. Each morning I got dressed then went downstairs until she was ready to go. We had gotten dressed and undressed in front of each other for all these years, and now we couldn't.

Although we both had a great time at the event and coming home with Dana and Laura, the weekend did nothing for our relationship. After we dropped them off and headed to her apartment, I could feel she was uncertain about what was going to happen when we got there and that I might talk about us being together again. We unloaded the car, and she kept saying there was no need for me to take her stuff up to the door. When everything was right outside the door, she turned to me said she had a nice time and gave me the shortest and least emotional kiss I'd ever received. From this point forward, our being together would only be at my request. She would go to keep me on an emotionally even keel and to appease me, not because she wanted to spend any time as a couple.

May was going to be a tough month for us. Both of our birthdays and anniversary were that month. Renee went home early in the month, and that was a relief. With Renee at home, she wanted our contact cut back. I didn't understand how not talking could be good for our situation. If lack of communication was one of the problems, this made no sense. I wanted us to talk, see each other, and try and find something to build on. She wanted to have as much freedom as possible and no connection to me. We did talk, but it was always difficult to have a simple conversation, but I kept trying.

Many of the things she said I never did for her I made every effort to now. Every chance I got to do something nice for her, I did; anything I thought she needed I got for her. To her it only seemed I was doing these things to hold on to her. That was not the reason. I was trying to show her that many of the things she wanted me to change I had and to give the relationship a chance. Her response was that I was going overboard and it would take time to see if the changes were real. Maybe I did too much at first, and there was merit in the wait-and-see approach, but if you didn't see each other, how would you know?

I was still having problems functioning each day. At times I would break down and then gain my composure to do a closing or a presentation. The people at my insurance job found out early on about my situation because one day while at the copier I simply began to cry and couldn't move. That may seem embarrassing to some people, but I just didn't care, and there was nothing at the time I could do about it. From that point on, they were there for me at every low point and offered sincere understanding and compassion.

The closing company didn't find out until later due to the fact I felt it would be better for them if they didn't have to worry about me. I could do this job in my sleep and still do it well, so I didn't want to burden them with my problems. They have been great men to work for and continue to be that way. They understood that the hours and time had put a strain on my marriage, but it was the nature of our business.

May 15 would be our thirty-third anniversary and my fifty-third birthday. Knowing it would be a difficult day for me, she asked if I wanted to go to lunch to celebrate my birthday. When I showed up, I brought a white rose to symbolize friendship and chocolate-covered almonds, which were her favorite. As I walked toward her desk, you could see she was unhappy I had brought her anniversary gifts. I explained thirty-three years was a great accomplishment and shouldn't be ignored but celebrated whatever the circumstances. She took the gifts, said thank you, and we went to have a pleasant lunch. She brought me a large bag of M&Ms, which are my favorite. When I took her back, she gave me a hug said, "Happy birthday," and went in but never once said anything about our anniversary.

That night, as always, the family went out for dinner to celebrate my birthday. We have a tradition in our family that we all go out together whenever it is someone's birthday. Besides my children, Terry and Monica, both my sisters, and their husbands, along with my brother's significant other, Beverly, were all joining us for dinner. My sisters have been very special to me through this entire ordeal. I called each one many times when I was depressed and unable to function. They were able to console and comfort me many times in a way that perhaps only siblings can do.

Right before dinner I got a call from her. She wished me a happy birthday and told me that she wanted me to have a nice evening. It seemed strange for her not to be there, and once again I wondered if this was going to be my life.

Eleven days later her birthday rolled around. I wanted desperately to take her for lunch. Figuring the girls where she worked would take her out, I just called to wish her a happy birthday and asked if anyone was going to lunch with her. She wasn't sure anyone was going to be able to go, and I suggested that we go together. She promised to call if no one went. After lunch, I called about something else, and she said no one had gone with her that day but that they were going another day. It hurt that she didn't let me take her on that day, but it was another example of her wanting to distance herself from me.

During this time, a friend who we graduated with came in from Alaska. He, her, and Dana were going to dinner to talk about our thirty-fifth class reunion. When I found out that I wasn't invited, I completely lost it. This would have been something we would have done together, and I didn't get an invitation to dinner or to join them. This was something once again that I was being left out of because we were not together. When I got her on the phone, I was so upset I'm sure I made very little sense. Seeing how upset I was, she told me to come by and see them and have a drink when I got back in to town. By the time I got to the restaurant, I was fine, and seeing her always calmed me down. After they finished dinner, we went over to a club that Dana was working at to visit more about old times.

When we left, I took her back to her car at the other restaurant. I asked if we could go to our class reunion together since most of the people there would not know about our situation. She said that she didn't think it would be a good idea but would think about it. I should have let it go at that, but I couldn't and didn't. I keep saying there was no reason why we shouldn't go together. They were classmates of both of us, and I really wanted us to do this together. The more I pleaded, the more frustrated she got. Finally she got in her car and drove off. My mind snapped at that point. This was not over, and we were going to settle it tonight. I chased her down the road until she had to pull over. I jumped out of the car and went to her window. I was out of control again, stating over and over that this wasn't right or fair.

She knows I would never physically hurt her, but she is still unsure about my temper. The window never came down all the way as she kept telling me she didn't want to go with me. Each time I heard those words it only upset me more and made me more determined that we go together. Once again she rolled up the window and drove away. I then did something I only did once and should never have done. I followed her all the way home. I have been embarrassed about my action to this day. Seeing that I was behind her, she pulled into the parking lot next to her apartment, and the window came down part way again. This talk would last for almost two hours as I tried to get her to explain why this was happening to us. It was ground we had covered more than once, but I only wanted either an explanation I could understand or another chance. I got neither. We didn't go to the reunion together.

In between this and the reunion, there was Memorial Day. Some years we would have people over for a cookout on this holiday. I called some of our friends and family to come over to visit with me and the kids. I told her we were all getting together and that she should come and spend time with the family. Thinking it would be mostly my family, she decided not to attend. Several of our friends were there, and after she found out they came, she regretted not coming. Another holiday and she was still gone, but it hadn't got any easier for me.

The reunion was June 6. These were the kinds of functions I excelled at. The bigger the crowd, the better I seemed to be. Several times I thought about not going. I knew it would be hard to be around her and not be with her, but our friends from Shreveport were coming up, and there would be a lot of people I would want to see. She was in charge of the decorations and setting up the event. Everything she picked out was right on target as usual. I went early to help her and Dana, who was in charge of the music. After everything was set up and we were ready to start, I asked if we could dance that evening, and she said that would be fine. Everything went well as we both visited with old friends and sat at different tables. I was pretty active in high school, so several stories were told about me and all the girls I was in love with at one time or another.

After dinner, the dancing began, and I thought we would perhaps have the first dance for old time's sake and because I had helped her with the decorations and set up. But once again we didn't have the same thought process. When the fifth dance was over, she finally came and asked me to dance. Maybe my emotions wouldn't let me see this all subjectively, but I thought it was wrong I had to wait that long to dance with her. I told her that I didn't really like the song and to wait. At that point, I got Melody and Tom, and we left to go to Halftime, a local sports grill. She seemed upset that we were leaving early, but what could she do? She said we hadn't danced yet to which I answered that five songs played before she thought of me, so it must not have been that important to her, which it wasn't. After the reunion was over, she showed up at Halftime, and we did have a dance.

The month of June was a terrible month as we dealt with my emotional rollercoaster and her wanting nothing to do with me. Many times I called her upset about something. I was overreacting to many of the events that happened. I could not control what I thought or what I did. Everything was a crisis when it came to her. More than once she tried to get me to back off and give us the time and space she said we needed. I couldn't do it. I knew I had lost her, and every little thing magnified that. We argued about almost everything at this point, but I would give in almost every time and then ask her to forgive me. It had become the dance we played. She would do something. I would get upset and act poorly then ask for forgiveness. There are other stories about me during this time, but they might involve other people, so I'll tell you again this time was not my shining moment and I am not proud of my behavior.

July 4 came, and the Baker family was coming over as usual. I asked her if she wanted to come and see everyone, but she said she was going to go out of town with the girls. She didn't even want me to know where or who she was going with on the trip. Supposedly she and the ladies she worked with went to San Antonio, but I have often wondered if that was where she really went. So much of what she told me was not all true or was flat-out untrue. She would try to hide things from me because she said she wasn't sure how I would react. I would usually find out and be upset, but if she had been straight with me, perhaps my reaction would not have been as bad as finding out other ways. Telling me the truth about what was going on was something I felt I deserved. She didn't think anything was my business and told me as little she could and never the whole truth.

There were many running phone battles during this time with things said mostly by me that I still cry about and ask for forgiveness. To explain the way I felt is not only impossible but futile. I couldn't figure out how to act or what to say when I was with her, and she wanted me to be around as little as possible. Whatever I did, it never seemed to be the right thing.

It had been five months since she told me she wanted out of the marriage, but I hoped that she would give us at least an opportunity to work things out. I still never knew what she was doing or with whom. We were married, so I didn't want to date or have her going out with other people until everything was final. In July, I found out she had begun a relationship with someone, and that began the end for me and the marriage.

THE DIVORCE

Once I found out she had developed a relationship with someone else, I again got out of control. I called and called asking how she could do this while we were still married? Her answer was always the same: it was none of my business and we were married only legally, not physically or emotionally. I couldn't at the time see any way to justify her being with someone else while married to me. It was hard to accept that she wanted to be with another person, but to do it while we were married I will always feel was wrong.

At this point, I decided to go ahead and get the divorce. At first she hesitated, saying I was upset and needed time to think it through, but when I said no, this was what I wanted, she said fine with no other argument. I explained that I couldn't see other people and be married, and if that was what she wanted, then we needed to end the marriage. She said someone at work had all the papers we would need; she would put it all together and let me know when I could look them over.

I had prayed every day for a miracle to come and save us. Of course it never came. She called to say the paperwork was filled out and that I could come over and look it over. I went over on a Sunday morning and sat with her at the table. As I read the terms of the divorce and the settlement between us, all I could think was, *Does thirty-three years of a marriage come down to who has to pay for what?* It was all spilt up according to her as a 50/50 deal. Sound familiar? There wasn't anything I didn't agree with it except maybe the $10,000 kitchen-remodeling bill I got because I was keeping the house. When she decided to go, I told her I wasn't selling the house. If she wanted to leave, she had to walk away, and I kept the house, so I suppose it was fair. I never wanted to spend that much on the remodel. It is a good-looking kitchen, but in the long run I probably won't get my money back.

Looking at the papers seemed to finalize where I was at that moment in my life. If my memory is correct, I held things together that day. I again asked her not to do this, but there was no changing her mind in the beginning or that day. There was one thing I asked for that day. If I was going be divorced, then I wanted the past to be in the past. Whatever had happened in our marriage before could not be brought up against me in the future. The marriage was ending, so we had to start new with each other. It is never easy to forget the past, and she remembered everything, so I didn't want my future relationship—if there was one—to be damaged by the former events or behavior. I needed a clean slate. She agreed we would bury things behind us and move forward but reminded me it could be years before she thought about having any relationships with me.

The next step would be to sign off and file the papers. In Oklahoma, you file a petition asking for the divorce, and then you go before a judge for the final degree. She didn't have the money for the filing, so I gave her a check to cover the cost. It was a busy time for her, so she said that she would file the papers the first part of the next week. We were going to go to lunch on Tuesday, but I was busy so we couldn't go. She would go with me to lunch to help keep me calm during this time.

Wednesday evening I was at a restaurant eating dinner and reading the paper when I came across something that put me into a state of near hysteria. When I read the paper, I read everything from cover to cover. I hadn't read the paper as much lately with all that was going on, but for some reason, I picked it up that day. As I read the public records under divorces asked for, there were our names. Seeing something in print can have an impact on people both positive and negative. Since I didn't think she was even filing for another week, I couldn't believe my eyes. I became so upset that a manager and several people came to see if I was all right and asked if I needed to have them call for help. She had gone on Monday and filed the papers but didn't realize they would put the filing in the paper. She thought she had to call and tell the paper and not that it was automatically recorded as public record.

When I called her, I was as upset as at any point during the ordeal. How could she file and not tell me? She told me she was going to tell me at lunch that

Tuesday, but we didn't go. Thinking it wouldn't be in the paper, she would tell me later. As usual, I found out anyway and went to pieces. I had an appointment that evening and needed to calm down, so she stayed on the phone until I was under control.

Thursday I called and told her to come over and pick up the divorce papers and to get a court date as soon as possible. She came over either that night or the next to pick up the papers and some of the pictures and other family things I thought she would like to keep. As I put everything on the table for her to see, I began to break down again. By the time she arrived, I was crying uncontrollably. I had several pictures of us and asked to take one that I like especially and put it with some letters I had written. I remember signing the papers and her holding me for a while so I could compose myself. It was dinner time, so we decided to go and have supper together. It may seem strange that we would sign divorce papers and then go out to eat, but she knew I needed to be with her, and so we went. Dinner, as usual, was fine, as if nothing was wrong.

Court dates could be on Monday, Wednesday, or Thursday. I told her to make arrangements to go on Wednesday. She called back to say her boss wanted her to do it on Thursday. I was getting a divorce I didn't want, and I couldn't even pick the day! I have no idea what I did the first three days of that week except I got her a newer 42-inch TV and took it to her. This was an uncontested divorce where both parties had agreed to everything, so there was no need for me to go. Everyone from my children, family, friends, and her didn't want me to be there. Once again I couldn't think like everyone else; I couldn't get divorced and not go to the proceedings. At the first of the week, I called her to make arrangements for that day.

Our court time was in the afternoon, but we had to go early to file papers for the divorce and a quit-claim deed on the house. She had told me several weeks before that she needed a cheese grater, so that morning I got up early and went to the store to get her a nice one. I picked her up at ten and gave her a white rose for friendship and the grater, and off to the courthouse we went to end our marriage.

When we arrived the first stop was at the county clerk's desk to file the papers. As we stood in line, a lady asked if we were there together. Since our court time was not till one thirty, I said, "Well, we are till then." It got a nervous chuckle from everyone, but I thought it was funny. We filed everything; then there was nothing left to do until the court time, so we went to drop off papers at the credit union and went to lunch.

We had an Italian restaurant that we ate at quite often downtown close to the courthouse, so we went there. It was a bit nostalgic and comforting all at the same time. So many memories came to me as I sat there having a pleasant conversation with the woman I was about to be divorced from that I wonder how I made it through the lunch without breaking down. My thoughts included family dinners there, a company Christmas party, and dozens of lunches with her. Yet we sat and talked like two old friends and as if nothing was wrong between us. She was concerned that I wouldn't make it through the day without getting emotional, and she didn't want to deal with that on this day if it got out of control, so I was doing everything I could to stay calm and relaxed.

After dining for about one and a half hours, we headed back to the courthouse. The proceedings were in a small court downstairs next to a convenience store with some tables. She sat with me until it was time to go in; then I waited outside for my life to end with her and change forever. I tried so hard not to cry, but I just couldn't stop the tears. Alone, I sat there still asking all the questions of why this was happening to us. Was it all so bad living with me? Was I such a terrible person that she couldn't bear to be with me? Had I failed her so badly that she had to find another life?

As usual, she had everything filled out perfectly, and the judge complimented her on the paperwork then granted the divorce. As she came out the door, she could see I was barely holding on, and as she reached me, I asked if we were done, and she said it was over. She held on to me for a while then said we needed to go upstairs again to record the papers. This would be the last time we would hold hands. I always thought our hands fit so well together, and I knew I would miss this forever. I had composed myself by the time we reached the clerk's office again and winked at the ladies that were there earlier in the day.

After leaving the courthouse, we decided to stop at a drive-in for an ice cream. We sat out on the patio and talked about small things and a little about how our lives would be from this point. I told her again that I wanted to see her and that I still wanted a chance to be with her, but she politely said, "No, not right now. Maybe later."

We still needed time and space away from each other. I told her as much as I loved her, I would look to be with other people, and she said that she not only understood but wanted me to. I took her home, and we gave each other a final hug and a small kiss, and I left.

That night was karaoke night at a grill that we all were going to each week. Our friend Dana does the karaoke, and my son and I sing songs together. Craig does numbers by himself and is very talented, so his mother comes out to hear him sing. That night she was there as usual and sitting at the table with us. We had decided to always greet each other with a friendly hug and be pleasant around our family and friends. This was never hard then, and it still isn't today. That night we closed the place down and had a wonderful evening together.

When I tell people about this day, they always think I have lost my mind. People who get divorced, they say, don't act that way. Through this whole process, I have tried to let my heart and conscience be my guide as much as I could and to act the way I felt was best for the both of us in the long run. It is strange, funny, and a little sad that one of the nicest days I ever had with my former wife was the day we divorced.

NOBODY ASKED ME, AND I DIDN'T HAVE A CHOICE

The reason I chose this title is because it is true. I never wanted a divorce, and she didn't give me a choice. I didn't get the chance to decide how our relationship would end or be during the process and afterward. I was married one day and for all practical purposes without a wife the next. This was always one of the hardest parts about ending the marriage. I wasn't allowed to know anything about her life after the night she told me those words. How does one just stop being a part of someone's life in one day? Do you really expect them to just not care about you anymore? I never understood how she could expect me to let the feelings and emotions I felt for her go so quickly.

As we went through the ordeal, everyone had his or her own brand of advice. People who had been divorced offered all kinds of advice and suggestions to both of us. Our divorce was different from almost any other divorce I have ever heard of. We both care a great deal for the other person, and although she wanted the marriage to end, I never once thought she deliberately hurt me, and I believe that today. I was hurt many times, but mostly because she either didn't think things through or only saw it from her perspective.

Many times she acted in a way that would cause me to become upset, or some days my emotions would simply not let me function. My children, sisters, and friends always did their best to calm me down, but in the end, she would be the only one who could. It is ironic that the one person who put me in this mess was the only person who kept me from going insane. I called her many times overreacting to something that had happened or upset me because of something she had done. Usually I would say something that I regretted and would later have to call and apologize. She always took my call. She would say she understood that I was upset and that she knew I didn't really mean what I said but that it hurt that I said it anyway. It will take time for me to forgive myself for the hurtful things I said. I have told her many times that I will always love her for being there for me each time. She has told me that she has forgiven me, and I hope and pray that is true.

In the first chapter, I asked the question, how did it all come to this? This is for me perhaps a rhetorical question, one that I can't answer objectively. There was indeed blame to go around to both parties. Was there really so much wrong with our marriage that it couldn't be fixed? Some people grow apart or change in ways that make them different from the people they were when they married, and maybe it is better that they part. People become disappointed that the person they married never lives up to their expectations, so they leave. They marry for the wrong reasons and finally one day walk away. Did any or all of these things happen to us? I have never been able to answer those questions. Perhaps you can.

Could the words "I don't love you" and "I never really loved you" be true? I don't believe anyone could be married to someone for thirty-three years and not be in love with them at some point in the marriage if not most of it. The first time I heard those words it hurt, but it really sunk in the next day. If she had never loved me, had I wasted all these years only to end up alone? How does someone live with someone for that long and then just leave them with nothing emotionally. I believe and will always believe she loved me but couldn't see spending the rest of her life in the position she thought we would be in forever.

You can't look into someone's eyes with their arms around you telling you that they love you and then say it back without meaning it for that long. When we said, "I love you," I usually said it first, but she always said it back and with sincerity and feeling. Even at the end, before those words came out, she would come to my room, tenderly kiss me each morning, and say, "I love you," and, "Good-bye." Can one do that and not have feelings for that person? I will never really know what she felt for me, and neither will she I believe. I was perhaps not the Prince Charming of her life nor the one great love she missed out on, but I did love her as much as I believe anyone could love someone.

She told me in the end that she felt she had settled for me. She should have waited and not rushed into getting married because I had convinced her it was the thing to do. I'm sad she felt that way. Settling means you married someone below you, and I always thought of us as equals. We each had our strengths and weakness that we brought to the marriage, and I never once thought I had under-married, regardless of our differences.

So much in my life was going to change, and I neither wanted nor asked for any of it to happen, but I was given no choice because it was what she wanted to do. What about what I wanted? I wanted a fifty-year wedding anniversary, family get-togethers, to play with our grandchildren together, and to enjoy my older years with the woman I loved, yet I was told I could have none of these things, and I had no choice in the matter. Life is unfair, they say, and these things happen. Well, does that make it right or just for both parties? She wanted to go, so she got to go no matter what. I have never understood this. Many times in a divorce someone is left miserable while the other seems to find happiness. Does one person's happiness outweigh that of the other person? There are those who say you need to do what will make you happy, but to what expense of another's happiness is that allowed? Why wasn't my happiness a consideration in the matter.

Did all of us have to be put through this so that she could have a life that she thought would make her happy? I have never wanted her to be unhappy for one day. I wanted her to be my wife and here with me and our children and grandchildren. Family has always been an important aspect of my life, and she took that away from me without my permission. We would have to figure out what to do about Thanksgiving, Christmas, and every other holiday from that point forward and who goes where on each holiday. Could we all be together? These were all questions that would have to be answered. Yet, nobody asked me if this was the way I wanted it. I don't want to sound bitter, but I want it understood this was not what I wanted, not what I thought I deserved, and that I had no choice.

When we got the divorce, her relationship with the children was strained to say the least. They had not been to her apartment and had minimal contact with her. It saddened me to see her missing out on so much with our family and for her to lose this time with the children and the grandsons. She had always wanted to be a mother and a grandmother, but that changed for her in some ways. I tried to get the children to have a relationship that was better with their mother; both sides wanted me to stay out of this matter. Because I felt sorry for her, I couldn't do it at first and still struggle with it to this day. The children never took sides in the matter. They simply felt it was better for me not to be married to their mother. When we separated, not one of the children asked me to try and reconcile with their mother. Although Renee felt we should stay married, she never thought it would be best for me to be with her.

Each of the children had asked me before why I stayed married to her years before this all went down. I always told them that although Mom could be difficult to live with, I loved her and wanted to be with her. They never once asked their mother this question. I may have said this before, but I'll say it one more time. My children love their mother. They just didn't always like her, and that is sad. I never really knew this until the separation, and I realize I failed them and their mother in this regard. As their father and her husband, there must have been something I could have done through the years that could have brought them closer together.

With time, I'm sure the relationships will heal. I know on my part that I made it more difficult for them because of my emotional state. They care a great deal for both of us, but I was the one in pain and distraught. There would be no way to tell you what Christy, Renee, and Craig meant to me as I went through this time. Many times I wish I could have handled all of this better and they didn't have to be there as often as they were. The times they talked to me and comforted me are what got me through. We have great kids, and we have always been proud of them and are so today. I love them and only wish I could have been a better father.

For my part, I can only say how sorry I am this happened to the both of us. Our lives will be forever changed. Two people for whatever reason were joined in holy matrimony and then told by a judge that they were no longer husband and wife. I know I will look back in time and have the proper perspective on this matter, but for now, I only feel regret, sadness, loneliness, and a deep sense of failure. It is easy to say if I could go back in time I would do things differently, but nothing could be more be true for me.

I would have romanced her in the beginning and throughout the marriage, thought of her feelings at all times, talked to her in a way that brought us closer, been the husband and man I could have been for her, and found a way to bring faith into our marriage. Mostly I would have made sure she knew I loved her more than anything else because she told me more than once she was never sure that was true.

Where was I to go from here? What was I to do? How would I survive? All these questions I asked myself for months. What happened after the divorce is not what this book is about. These and other issues would come into play with my life—issues I never thought I would have to deal with, but nobody asked me, and I didn't have a choice.

EPILOGUE

I don't cry anymore. There was a time before last Halloween that I cried every day and some days all day long. It has been two years since the divorce and eight months since I finished the book. My life has changed in many ways and stayed the same in others. I'm not the person I was before, but I am a better person. At the core I'm still Rickey Carr.

Faith has become more important to me and my former wife has begun to attend church. I know that we should have done that together because it was something we missed out on as a couple. We both believed; we just never shared it with each other. Church and prayer has been a great comfort to me. When Renee had the accident and then recovered, it was a miracle and a blessing that strengthened my personal beliefs. I told someone it was sometimes hard to remember to pray when it hadn't been part of a daily routine. But it is my goal each day to begin with a prayer.

My children are still wonderful and my grandsons are a joy. It still bothers me that we don't share this part of our life together. She will see them one weekend and I'll go the next. There are times we do things together, but it is not the same feeling of enjoyment. Her relationship has improved with the children. Personally I wish it was better than it is, but I try not to voice an opinion because both sides would rather I leave it up to them. They have gone to her apartment for dinner and they are both coming to peace with one another.

One of the companies I worked for went out of business and the other one I couldn't concentrate on enough due to my mental state, so I had another career change. The job market has completely passed me by at fifty-four. Everything is now on the internet. I was old-school and the world was full of technology I had no idea how to use. Many of the companies I applied for required a college degree. I was unable to get an interview for the things I was qualified for and ready to step into. After weighing all my options, I went back to finish my degree. I enrolled in a fast-track adult program and have enjoyed the experience. Going to class one night a week with students much younger than I has been invigorating. If I had made the grades in school that I am making now, my parents would have been very proud. Now I am.

The single world has its own set of challenges. Dating is a whole new world. There are internet dating, speed dating, dating services and a host of web sites to find someone. I have dated some very charming women. Several I met on the internet, one through a dating service, one at a club and another through a mutual friend. There are certain phrases you learn quickly such as baggage, history and red flags. Single people seem to gravitate to clubs. I have learned to two-step, waltz, and line-dance while improving my dancing. If you're going to go out, learning to dance is the best way to socialize. Men are afraid of being turned down; but if you watch who goes out to the floor and ask them to dance, there is a good chance they will say yes. Being a bad dancer is no excuse; find someone and let them teach you, go to free lessons and practice. It's more fun on the floor than just standing there all night doing nothing but holding a drink.

My former wife and I see each other at many of the places we go to. It has gotten easier for me to be around her without actually being with her because I understand the boundaries; I don't like them, but I understand them. My feelings for her are still very strong and that makes it difficult for her at times to deal with me. I couldn't turn off my feelings like a light switch, which is what she wanted. I have no idea if we will ever get back together. We go to dinner on occasion, but we still don't date. We still always answer each other's calls and texts. Since the divorce we have both helped each other in many ways due to the fact that we care a great deal for each other and always will, I believe.

Being alone is something I'm still getting used too. There are so many things I miss doing with someone. I miss having a person to kiss good night and good morning, hearing the words "I love you," playing with the grandsons together, eating dinner and having a conversation about each other's day and building memories. The life I have now is not a bad life, just not the one I wanted. Each day I think about what might have been, but it doesn't eat at me the way it did in the beginning. I still have many unanswered questions and struggle with the fact that our marriage ended.

She seems to be happy, but only she can really say. Recently she told me that she felt alone during our marriage because of my job and my leaving her on Sunday to play golf. She felt she might as well be alone and live her life the way she wanted if she was going to feel lonely anyway. Sadly, Sunday is the hardest day for me. When I told her that perhaps it was my penance, she agreed with me. I never wanted her to feel that way and I am truly sorry.

Someone told me I should write this epilogue to help other people going through this experience and show that there is hope. People have a lot of advice when you go through a divorce. What I can tell you is this; always do what your heart tells you is right. When you get up in the morning all the people that gave advice are gone, but you have to look in the mirror. I did a lot of things people thought were crazy before and after the divorce, but I always did what I thought would be best for her and my family in the long run. The next piece of advice is to be nice. It may seem simple to say that, but just be nice. No matter how you have been wronged, always be nice. This is the main reason we still talk and care for each other today. Many times we hurt each other; however we never meant to be mean or spiteful. When I have told people this they appear to be shocked. Why would I be nice to someone who wronged me? First, it is the

Christian thing to do. If you don't believe, then it is still the right thing to do.

I survived and I'm a better person today. It is tragic that I had do go through this to become what I could and should have been all along. I work hard and up to my ability each day, apply myself at school and take care of things in a timely manner. I have found my faith and enjoy many things I never did before. You may believe, as I did, that your pain will never go away. And maybe it will never completely be gone. But in those times, just do what I did; take a moment, bow your head and say a prayer. It worked for me.